DIESELS & ELEC

LOCOMOTIVES INTERNATIONAL SPECIAL EDITION No. 1

A Locomotives International Publication

Above: On New Zealand's North Island a long Wellington to Auckland goods train crosses the Hapuawhenua Viaduct near Ohakune hauled by a new class "Df" English Electric 1,500 hp 2-Co-Co-2 diesel electric locomotive. New Zealand Railways publicity photograph, circa 1954.

Front Cover: One of 15 class S1 Bo-Bos built by Brush and exported to Cuba in 1968-69, no. 2732 works on the 3 foot gauge railway serving the Hermanos Ameijeiras sugar mill, where it was photographed in February 2001. Photo: Peter Smith.

Title Page: Hedjaz Railway teak-bodied DeDion Bouton railcar no. ACM 3 stands in the station at Derra'a shortly after an overhaul, on 9th October 2002. Photo: Wolfgang Ewers.

ISBN 1-900340-16-X
First Edition. Published by Paul Catchpole Ltd., The Haven, Trevilley Lane, St. Teath, Cornwall, PL30 3JS, Great Britain.
www.locomotivesinternational.co.uk
Printed and bound by Image Design & Print, Bodmin, Cornwall, Great Britain.
British Library Cataloguing in Publication Data. A catalogue record for this book is available from the British Library.

Diesels and Electrics
Locomotives International

Contents

Acknowledgements:

The collective authors of this edition are, in alphabetical order: Paul Catchpole, Keith Chester, Paul Engelbert, Wolfgang Ewers, Mario Forni, Ray Gardiner, Roger Hennessey, P.M. Kalla-Bishop, Nicholas Pertwee, Peter Smith, Ian Thomson, Gottfried Wild.

In addition to the principal authors of the various chapters several photographers have provided extra illustrations and their names are credited in the captions to their pictures. Uncredited photos in each chapter are either the principal author's or have been selected from the principal author's collection.

Introduction

While every last puff of smoke has been recorded as steam locomotives retire around the world, other forms of traction have been largely overlooked.

An early generation of diesels from the 1920s and 1930s has virtually gone with the exception of a few rare examples surviving in scattered locations. Even museum exhibits from this period are relatively uncommon. The post-war diesel generation, contemporaries of the classes produced during the BR modernisation plan are less rare but rapidly disappearing, outside of preserved collections. Narrow gauge locomotives from this era can likewise still be found at work but by the nature of the agricultural or industrial concerns that operate them these locos are less well known or recorded than their main line counterparts, and often less accessible to enthusiasts.

Electric traction has fared a little better as electric locomotives tend to be longer-lived and more veterans have remained at work into recent times. Nevertheless, there are large areas that remain undocumented, even unknown, to the average enthusiast - and by that I am not just referring to the more ancient locomotives.

As soon as the suggestion was made to create a special edition on 'modern traction' (for want of a more appropriate term - there's not much 'modern' about the traction in this book!) many of our regular contributors showed an immediate enthusiasm and prepared articles on subjects in which they had a particular interest or into which they had already been researching. Added to these are a few items on file that had been awaiting publication and various photographs in the archives.

The result of the quantity and quality of material submitted is this volume and another to follow. They will hopefully start to redress the balance between steam and other forms of motive power in railway history publications. In the future the bias towards steam might otherwise be seen as causing a gap in the recording of railway history, which it would be better to plug now while the relevant people and locomotives are still around.

This book is only a glimpse into the subject, though a few specific areas are looked at in detail. There must be much more to see before coverage of diesels and electrics around the world matches that of steam. Perhaps some readers will be inspired to probe a bit further or even pack their suitcases. As holidays take us to more exotic locations, just recording what is seen helps.

The collective authors of this edition:

Paul Catchpole: Editor and publisher of 'Locomotives International' books and magazines. Before becoming involved with the magazine he had written 'The Steam Locomotives of Czechoslovakia' and is now sourcing and translating material for a similar work on diesel and electric locomotives and railcars.

Keith Chester: Author and editor of 'East European Narrow Gauge' and of several books about Russian steam locomotives. Based in Vienna, Keith Chester has researched and written about railways in central and eastern Europe and is well known for his work in this area.

Paul Engelbert: Author of 'Forestry Railways in Hungary' and 'Schmalspurig durch Bulgarien' (Stenvalls Forlag), Dutchman Paul Engelbert has travelled throughout central and eastern Europe in search of narrow gauge railways.

Wolfgang Ewers: One of the contributors to 'Steam and Rail in Germany', Wolfgang Ewers has written about other matters in the magazine, including an article giving an insight into the German involvement in a railway across the Sahara that was never completed.

Mario Forni: An author known in Italy for writing about railways in his local Trento area, Mario Forni also has wider interests which have resulted in contributions to 'Locomotives International', drawing on his own photographs and others in his archive collection.

Ray Gardiner: An enthusiast with a particular interest in sugar mill railway systems. Living in Australia has enabled Ray Gardiner to visit parts of south-east Asia, especially Indonesia, as well as travelling further afield to visit Cuba's mills.

Roger Hennessey: Author of 'Atlantic: the Well Beloved Engine' and other books not only about railways but also scientific matters. A contributor to various journals and working on a history of the Royal Engineers' construction of the Trans-Caucasian Railway.

P.M. Kalla-Bishop: A late author of international repute, well known for his books on Hungarian and Italian Railways.

Nicholas Pertwee: Having spent much of his working life in the far east, Nicholas Pertwee has explored and photographed various railway locations in China, Japan and Taiwan, and has recently had an article on locomotives seen in North Korea published in the magazine.

Peter Smith: An enthusiast of Cuban railways who has looked at the national railway system as well as the well-known sugar mill lines. As a modeller of note too, Peter Smith's 'O' gauge Cuban railway has been featured in the 'Continental Modeller'.

Ian Thomson: By profession the United Nations Transport Consultant for South America and by inclination a railway historian and conservationist. Author of 'Red Norte' and many articles and a tireless worker for the benefit of South America's railways.

Gottfried Wild: A broad interest in all forms of traction combined with a love of research has resulted in authoritative accounts of many experimental projects. He also assisted with sourcing information and diagrams for 'The Railways of Romania' and has made other contributions to the magazine.

The World's First Main Line Diesel -
the Diesel-Klose-Sulzer "Thermolokomotive" *by Keith R. Chester*

By the first decade of the twentieth century the newly invented diesel motor had firmly established itself within the shipping industry. Rudolf Diesel, however, saw great potential (and presumably great profits) for his motor in railway locomotives and was keen to promote its development in this branch. To this end he formed the "Gesellschaft für Thermolokomotiven, Diesel, Klose, Sulzer GmbH" together with the Swiss-based Sulzer company and Adolf Klose. Sulzer already had considerable experience with the development and manufacture of marine diesel engines, whilst Klose, one of the most talented locomotive engineers of his generation, devoted most of his energies after the turn of the century to the promotion of diesel motors.

The Diesel-Klose-Sulzer "Thermolokomotive" on trial, possibly in Switzerland. Photo: Author's collection.

The new company initially worked on a number of paper projects in the hope of awakening the interest of private and state-owned railway companies in diesel locomotives. One such was a proposal for a main line 4-4-4 locomotive capable of hauling a 200t train at 90km/h on the level and at 50km/h up a grade of 1 in 100. This was accepted by the KPEV, a railway with a long tradition of being open to innovation and of carefully testing new designs, and in spring 1909 it placed an order for such a loco, the first large diesel-powered locomotive ever to be built. Sulzer supplied the motors and Borsig, under the direction of Klose, the mechanical parts, which were given Borsig works number 7409/1910. Rudolf Diesel was closely involved throughout the project.

The result was a locomotive 16.6m long, powered by a V-shaped four-cylinder engine developing 1250hp and driving the four coupled axles via a "Blindwelle". That the locomotive was three years in construction reflected the difficulties faced by the designers of this pioneering prototype. One problem which emerged was starting the loco under full load with the diesel motor. The solution chosen was to initially drive the motor with compressed air generated by a compressor powered by a small 250hp motor. Once a speed of 8-10km/h had been reached, the diesel motor would cut in.

The loco was assembled by Sulzer in Switzerland and its first trials were held in September 1912. The engine cooling system proved unsatisfactory and the "Thermolokomotive" was returned to the Sulzer works for modifications. These took some six months and it was not until March 1913 that further test runs took place on the Winterthur - Romanshorn line. These seem to have been satisfactory and on 31 March, the loco began a four-day journey to Berlin under its own power, mostly light engine, but it also double-headed two fast goods trains. On both occasions it briefly powered the train alone, reaching a maximum speed of 70km/h.

At the end of May 1913 the Grunewald Test Station near Berlin began testing the loco. However, as the "Blindwelle" broke during the third trial run on May 29, all testing was halted for another six months whilst this was renewed. Upon the resumption of trials the loco made six test runs with a load of 200t between 12 February and 6 March 1914. On the latter date a cylinder cracked, putting paid to any further testing. The loco was never to run again.

Unfortunately, on trial the loco had not lived up to expectations. There were problems with the 250hp motor, which proved incapable of providing sufficient compressed air, particularly on trials which included frequent stopping and starting, and the loco was compelled to stand while it produced enough to get it on the move again. Fuel consumption was high and the loco itself was extremely noisy. There were also grave concerns about the loco's lack of power, so much so that Grunewald refused to test it with a 300t train for fear of blocking a main line.

Whether these were all just teething troubles which could have been ironed out we shall never know. Certainly the engineers and founders of the Diesel-Klose-Sulzer Company were keen to continue working on the loco. But with the outbreak of war in August 1914, any interest the KPEV might once have had in the "Thermolokomotive" waned and the world's first main line diesel locomotive was soon scrapped.

Further technical details and diagrams are provided in the chapter 'Direct Drive on Diesel Locmotives'.

Early Diesel Traction Development *by Paul Catchpole*

What was the British diesel locomotive industry doing before the British Railways 1955 Modernisation Plan and how did it compare with what else was going on around the World? Although some companies hitherto not in the business of diesel traction turned their attention in that direction, others had already been building railcars and locomotives for 20-25 years and were exporting their products overseas.

When considering dieselisation, British Railways cast aside this considerable experience, claiming that there was nothing already available suited or adaptable to British conditions and proposed to test 147 different prototypes in order to find suitable designs to satisfy motive power in three power ranges. This ridiculous intention was never satisfied as the British Transport Commission was forced to act quickly and in 1957 ordered series production in four different power ranges, Classes 1, 2, 3 and 4. Caution was thrown to the winds and some of the locomotive types were ordered without any prototype at all.

Really, by this time BR could have just placed a bulk order with American locomotive producers for virtually off-the-shelf designs but that would not have been politically acceptable. In fact some of the locomotives that became well-known on BR bore a notable resemblance to others being exported around the Commonwealth and to South America, as we shall see. First though it is worth turning back to look some of the earlier work of the British diesel locomotive industry and how it related to events elsewhere.

From Petrol to Diesel

When World War One broke out the task of operating field railways to bring supplies forward to the trenches created a huge demand for narrow gauge locomotives. Most of this need was catered for by the large-scale production of standardised steam designs but of course the trails of smoke and steam left behind gave away their position to the opposite side. The diesel engine was not yet sufficiently well developed so the armies adopted petrol motors, already tried and tested for road transport, to power small locomotives to work close behind the lines. An example of one of these, a 4-wheel Motor Rail loco, is preserved at the Leighton Buzzard Narrow Gauge Railway.

After the Great War and through the 1920s petrol fuelled engines were employed in the development of rail-cars, small shunters and narrow gauge locomotives, worldwide. The Hedjaz Railway's DeDion Bouton railcar described in a later chapter is a classic example. Diesel engines were not to generally come into their own really

until the 1930s but development work resumed once the hostilities were over.

Diesel technology started to move ahead more quickly in the USA and Canada while in Europe, Germany and Russia were led by M.A.N. and the partnership of Esslingen and Lomonossof. Switzerland was prominent with the production of Sulzer engines, often installed in other manufacturers' designs.

Great Britain did not figure very much in the early days of diesels although the London & North Eastern Railway undertook some experiments with an Austrian-built locomotive in 1924. Marginally more successful was an LMS train temporarily converted from a Manchester-Bury electric set in 1928 by installing a 500 hp Beardmore engine and English Electric traction motors. It was to be another ten years before the LMS built their better known three-car articulated streamlined set.

Express Railcars in the 1930s

Greater success with diesel power was achieved by mounting the engines in railcars than in locomotives as the motors were not yet particularly powerful and also suffered from a poor ratio of weight to output. Initially progress was made by installing diesel motors in existing railcar designs, for example by the Hungarian Ganz company and Kralovopolská of Brno in Czechoslovakia.

The first British main line to successfully introduce diesel traction for public services was the LNER which took the lead in 1931 when the 'Tyneside Venturer' went into operation, followed

The early Hungarian branch line railcars were built with petrol motors from 1926 onwards but from 1929 Ganz started to install diesel engines. Fortunately some early examples of two-axle cars such as this class BCmot have been preserved in Budapest and are used for the shuttle from Keleti station to the Museum Park.

shortly by two further railcars of the same type.

The Great Western Railway turned to railcars a couple of years later, after a streamlined vehicle built by AEC in 1933 was shown at a London exhibition. Capable of carrying 70 passengers at 75mph (121 km/h), it went into public service in 1934 and formed the prototype for another 37 railcars, some adapted for special purposes. The GWR's vehicles were Britain's only real taste of the 1930s express railcar boom.

Far more significant in international terms were the 'Fliegender Hamburger' (Flying Hamburger) railcars that revolutionised passenger services between Berlin and Hamburg. The articulated two-unit diesel-electrics had been tested up to 175 km/h and were introduced on 15th May 1933 on a public schedule that required running at maximum speed of 160 km/h and an average of 125 km/h, a performance hitherto unheard of. Each half of the unit had a 410 hp motor and an electric generator mounted on the outer bogie but the drive was by traction motors on the central articulation bogie, either axle being supplied with electricity from the power unit on the nearer outer bogie. Seats were provided for 98 second class passengers and the railcars were equipped with a small buffet.

The improvements in diesel and transmission technology that had enabled this leap forward in diesel traction in the early 1930s soon spread to neighbouring countries. Classic examples are the Hungarian 'Arpad' and Czechoslovakian 'Modrý Šíp'. Particularly worthy of mention are the Danish 'Lyntog' (Lightning Train) units of 1935 that nearly doubled the average rail speed of a train and ferry journey from Esjberg to Copenhagen and which continued in service into the 1980s. The initial 3-car versions were powered by four 104 hp engines driving traction motors on all axles. They were designed to be able to continue operating in the event of an engine failing and maintenance was eased by the facility for simple dismounting and replacement of the engines.

Progress in Europe was matched by developments in America. In 1930 General Motors had bought up the Electro-Motive Company and Winton Engine Co., forming the basis of the EMD - Electro Motive Division. This was highly significant as GM applied the production philosophy already successful in road car production, which was to make standard designs available as mass production models at economical prices. This approach, on a worldwide scale, really accounted for the demise of the steam locomotive at least as much as the stagnation of steam technology

development, strangled by entrenched conservatism.

Several years of development resulted in the first of the light-weight American diesel railcars, a 3-car stainless steel set, the 'Pioneer Zephyr'. An inaugural run from Denver to the Century of Progress Exhibition in Chicago was made on May 26th 1934 at an average speed of 78 mph (125 km/h). The traction equipment included a 600 hp 2-stroke diesel engine generating electricity for a pair of nose-suspended traction motors to power the leading bogie.

The Union Pacific was also in the race to produce the first diesel-electric express railcar set. The M10000 3-car set appeared in February 1934 but as the intended diesel engine was not ready a spark-ignition motor was installed. When the M10001 6-car sleeper train was produced later in the same year it was possible to equip it with a 900 hp V-12 diesel engine, later substituted by a 1,200 hp V-16 engine, which powered four traction motors driving the axles of the two leading bogies. As with the Zephyr the engine was a 2-stroke model. On October 22nd this supremely ugly train broke the record for the 3,260 mile (5,216km) transcontinental crossing of the USA by making the journey in 57 hours, an achievement that remains unequalled.

Locomotive Development in Britain After World War One

As with railcars, progress on locomotives was mainly made in small steps with modest engines of meagre power output. Through the 1920s diesel power was applied to small shunters and narrow gauge locos, mostly with a mechanical transmission to rod-coupled driving wheels. During this period many of the companies that were to become today's manufacturers were making petrol-engined locomotives or non-railway industrial equipment while some were also steam loco builders. Several of the early diesel designs incorporated engines manufactured by J&H McLaren of Leeds who had taken out a manufacturing licence from the German Benz company.

Next door to McLaren's factory was Hudswell Clarke, who turned out their first diesel loco in 1927 (works no. P261) and exported it to a 2'6" gauge forestry railway in Burma. This was a small 30 hp 4-wheel loco tractor, but their next locomotive was altogether more ambitious.

The 'Junin' was also of 2'6" gauge but was a 32 ton, 300 hp 1-C-1 with transmission through a Sinclair fluid flywheel to a gearbox and jackshaft drive. The radiator alone weighed 3 tons! A 6-cylinder McLaren-Benz engine with Bosch solid fuel injec-

In 1932 Hawthorn Leslie built a pair of 2 foot gauge diesel-mechanicals for the Tokar-Trinktat Light Railway in the Sudan. They had to work in hot, dusty conditions and within a maximum axle load of only 5 tons had to incorporate an effective cooling system that included a 50 gallon auxiliary water tank as well as protection against the abrasive wind-blown sand for the McLaren engine and all the bearings. Transmission was through a three-speed gearbox with a worm reduction gear, claimed to be the first time such a gear was applied to railway traction. Ironically a small petrol engine was also fitted to the loco for the purpose of starting up the diesel engine. Their main duties were hauling 170-ton trains of cotton for which the maximum speed of just 10 mph (16 km/h) was presumably deemed sufficient. The locomotive shown in the publicity photo from 1933 was S.R. No. 55.

tion generated up to 12,550 lbs of tractive effort in second gear and was started from cold by compressed air. Built in 1930 for the Junin Railway on Chile's high plateau, the 'Junin' proved a great success and outlasted the nitrate industry for which it was built. The loco was found abandoned but perfectly preserved by the almost complete dryness of this region and was saved from a scrap merchant and repatriated in 1990 for preservation at the Armley Mill Museum, Leeds (to the subsequent disappointment of Chilean enthusiasts as 'Junin' was the first diesel locomotive in their country).

Kerr Stuart was another of the early producers of diesel locomotives, available from 1928 onwards in standardised 30, 60 and 90 hp versions with a mechanical transmission and chain drive. The prototype of the 60 hp locomotives (works no. 4415/1928) went to Mauritius to work on the Union Vale sugar estate but was repatriated to the Ffestiniog Railway in 1997. In fact this particular loco had initially been demonstrated on the Welsh Highland Railway and on the FR before a brief spell in Ireland. One of the 90 hp locos is also preserved, standard gauge no. 4428 of 1929, kept at the Buckinghamshire Railway Centre, Quainton.

The Hunslet Engine Co. bought out the liquidated remains Kerr Stuart in 1930 after the bizarre disappearance of its chairman and went on to produce many narrow and standard gauge diesels through the 1930s, a fair proportion of which were exported. The first of Hunslet's own standard gauge diesels, works no. 1697 of 1932, was exhibited at that year's British Industries Fair and then underwent extensive trials on the London Midland & Scottish Railway hauling heavy coal trains.

The following year the LMS decided to compare the variety of diesel shunters available by this time, and ordered nine locomotives from five manufacturers; Armstrong Whitworth (1), Drewry Car Co. (1), Harland & Wolff (1), Hudswell Clarke (2), and Hunslet (4). All locos had mechanical transmissions except for the Armstrong Whitworth which was a diesel-electric, but all the Hunslet locos differed in some way in their engine types and transmissions. The nine locos were numbered 7400-7408, renumbered almost immediately to 7050-7058. In 1940 nos. 7050-7054 were taken over by the army for use at various locations around Britain and were renumbered into the War Department series. Most received modifications of some sort and two have survived to be preserved. 7050 is at the Museum of Army Transport, Beverley, 7051 is at the Middleton Railway, Leeds.

LMS No.	WD No.	Maker	Type	Scrapped
7050	25	Drewry/English Electric	0-4-0	Preserved
7051	27	Hunslet	0-6-0	Preserved
7052	24	Hunslet	0-6-0	1969
7053	23	Hunslet	0-6-0	1954
7054	26	Hunslet	0-6-0	1974
7055	-	Hudswell Clarke	0-6-0	?
7056	-	Hudswell Clarke	0-6-0	?
7057	233	Harland & Wolff	0-6-0	1965
7058	-	Armstrong Whitworth	0-6-0	?

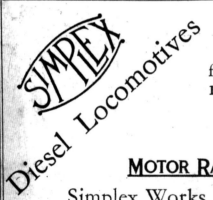

The 7051 design was sufficiently successful to be repeated for export to the Peruvian Corporation (ending up as F.C. Central of Peru no. 505), and with modifications to suit differing gauges also for the Egyptian Phosphate Co. and the Sinai Mining Co.

After the LMS trials it was decided that though some of the locos had acquitted themselves well, something more powerful was wanted and electric transmission was decided upon. Two batches of 350 hp 0-6-0D with jackshaft drive were built in 1935/36, ten by Armstrong Whitworth with Armstrong-Sulzer engines and ten by Hawthorn Leslie with English Electric

Above: No. 7050, designed by Drewry but built by English Electric.

Above: A publicity photo showing a line-up of some of the LMS diesels on trial. From left to right: 7051, 7056, 7055, 7054 & 7052.

Right: A builder's photo used for company advertising in the 1930s, showing one of the two Hudswell Clarke 0-6-0D as LMS no. 7055. Twenty years on British Railways ordered some remarkably similar shunters from the same company.

Harland & Wolff of Belfast used this picture taken inside their works for publicity too. The locomotive, named 'Harlandic', became LMS 7057 but was later loaned to the War Department for use at Sinfin Lane Depot, where it was numbered WD 233. In 1945 it was returned to the maker who rebuilt it with a 225 hp engine, raising the bonnet to the level of the cab roof. After regauging to 5'3" it was purchased by the Northern Counties Committee and worked in Northern Ireland until April 1965.

engines, LMS nos. 7059-7068 and 7069-7078 respectively. These twenty engines were the origin of today's class 08 shunters and other similar locomotives built for overseas railways. With the exception of nos. 7074 and 7076, all were taken into WD stock 1939-41. Most were used overseas but 7069 survived the war in France and was repatriated to the Swanage Railway in 1987.

The LMS in 1939 decided to combine the best design elements of the two batches and to undertake assembly in their own workshops. Armstrong Whitworth had by this time ceased diesel production but their mechanical design was adopted with installation of the English Electric motor. Many ended up over-seas working for the WD in the Middle East, North Africa and Italy and when the army required more diesels for D-Day they ordered them from the LMS. The incorporation of a jackshaft drive within the rigid wheelbase had caused problems so the opportunity was taken to improve the design by using two traction motors with double reduction gearing and a reduced wheel diam-eter. This was now virtually the class 08 diesel in its final guise.

After purchase of some ex-WD examples the Nederlands Staatsbahn also adopted the design as its standard shunter and had 115 similar examples built by English Electric. The ex-WD locos were NS 501-510, the post-war locos being 511-545 and 601-665, of which the latter batch were equipped with train brakes. One of the former WD locos, NS no. 508 is preserved at Utrecht.

Before continuing, we should go back to 1933 to mention some locomotives built for main line service for the LNER by Armstrong Whitworth, in fact the first British main line diesels. The design was a 1-C-1 mixed traffic type that could be run as single or multiple units and operate at speeds up to 70 mph (112 km/h). The power plant was an 8-cylinder Armstrong-Sulzer motor driving a generator to supply current to three Crompton Parkinson traction motors. Tractive effort of each single unit was estimated to be 28,500 lbs. Tests on assorted passenger and goods trains were undertaken on the Newcastle - Edinburgh and Carlisle routes prior to entry into service of the first locomotive on the Newcastle - Berwick part of the system.

British and European exports to Argentina and Thailand in the 1920s and 1930s.

Most attention tends to be focused on Europe and North America but diesel traction was in use in a number of countries elsewhere quite early on, Argentina being a particularly bold leader in the field using locomotives and railcars manufactured in Britain and Hungary. Thailand's metre gauge railways were also early users of diesel electrics, introducing Swiss and Danish built locos in 1931.

The first diesel in South America was a bogie railcar built by the Metropolitan Carriage & Wagon Co. for the Buenos Aires Great Southern Railway in 1929 and equipped with a 375 hp engine made in Scotland by Beardsmore. Another similar vehicle with a larger Sulzer engine followed. The following year Armstrong Whitworth supplied the first pair of 'power house' units, each with a pair of 600 hp Sulzer motors and Oerlikon generators, for coupling inside a 5-car railcar set equipped with traction motors on the coaches. So successful were they that not only were three more built for operating 8-car trains but electrifi-cation plans were abandoned. Furthermore a version of the 8-car 'power house' units was constructed as a 1,700 hp mixed traffic locomotive with a view to further examples being purchased with different gear ratios for passenger or freight haulage.

Armstrong Whitworth supplied Sulzer-engined diesel railcars to other railways in Argentina (and Brazil) through the 1930s but the largest order for British products went to Drewry for 99 broad gauge bogie railcars for the BAGSR and the Buenos Aires Western Railway and eight more shared between the Argentine North Eastern Railway and the Entre Ríos Railway, both of stan-dard gauge. These were all diesel-mechanicals, supplied 1936-37, but also in 1937 the Birmingham RC&W Co. supplied two diesel-hydraulic railcars with 120 hp Leyland engines to the Buenos Aires & Pacific Railway. The same railway built six bogie railcars with 240hp Ganz engines in their own works, three with mech-anical transmission and three with Voith-Sinclair transmission.

In 1936 the Argentine State Railway gave Ganz of Budapest a

This diesel shunter was photographed from a train window in 1972 at San Giuseppe di Cairo, Italy. It had been built by the LMS at Derby in 1941 and served in the Middle East as WD no. 55. It was moved to Tunisia in 1943 before transfer to Italy in 1944. The Italian State Railways (FS) purchased the loco in 1946, in company with three others that had also served with the Middle East Forces and numbered them Ne 700.001 - 004. WD 55 became 700.003 and worked until 1978 but remained in FS stock till 1984. The Ferrovie Sinalunga-Arezza-Stio bought the loco in 1991.

Photo: D. Trevor Rowe.

Armstrong Whitworth & Co. frequently publicised their diesel locomotive and railcar construction facilities through the 1930s. These two pictures from their adverts allow an interesting comparison to be made between the LNER 1-C-1 and the mixed traffic loco delivered to Argentina. Technical drawings reproduced to modellers scales on the following page show further detail.

large order for 3-car streamlined express railcars to upgrade services on the Central North, East and Patagonian systems. They were constructed in 1937 and arrived at the docks in Buenos Aires in August 1938. Each unit had two driving cars with a non-powered coach in the centre. The driving bogies at the outer ends were of A1A formation, each powered by a 320hp engine and mechanical transmission, giving a maximum speed in service of 110 km/h. During World War 2 maintenance became a problem but afterwards they were revitalised to operate some of Argentina's top passenger services through the Perón era.

Thailand's first diesel power consisted of two diesel-mechanical 0-4-0 jackshaft drive locos built in 1928 by SLM with 200 hp 6-cylinder engines. Their maximum speed was 40 km/h (25 mph) so they were mainly used as shunters and one was preserved after withdrawal in 1964. The success of these two locos led to the purchase of two types of main line diesel with differing wheel and drive arrangements, both built as a batch of six examples and intended for operation at 60 km/h.

The A1A-A1A diesel electrics were built in 1931 by Henschel with 450 hp Sulzer engines and Oerlikon electrical gear. They lasted at least 40 years in service. The other six were 2'Do2' types built in the same year by Frichs, each with a pair of their own 500 hp engines driving Oerlikon electrical equipment. With a power rating of 1,000 hp they were trusted with principal express duties but were allowed to become run down due to lack of main-

tenance during the Second World War and were withdrawn in the 1950s. No. 556 is preserved though. A 1,600 hp twin-unit 2'Do+Do2' version for goods trains was built in 1932 but the rigid frame types were not perpetrated as the bogie locos rode better and were kinder to the track.

By the mid 1930s many more railways around the globe were following the lead and British diesel locomotives and railcars were being exported for main line service in countries within the Empire and elsewhere. The home market, however, proved very hard to supply with main line diesel traction, though industrial users of shunting engines proved a little more flexible in outlook.

After the start of World War 2 little development was undertaken, though a long-lived series of 37 0-4-0DM deisgned by Andrew Barclay & Sons were supplied to the War Department by Barclay, Drewry and the Vulcan Foundry in 1941-42 and 1945. Many worked abroad for the forces and they are sometimes seen in pictures of the D-Day landings being hauled up the beach by caterpillar trucks. Eight examples survived in military ownership into the 1990s and some of these have been preserved.

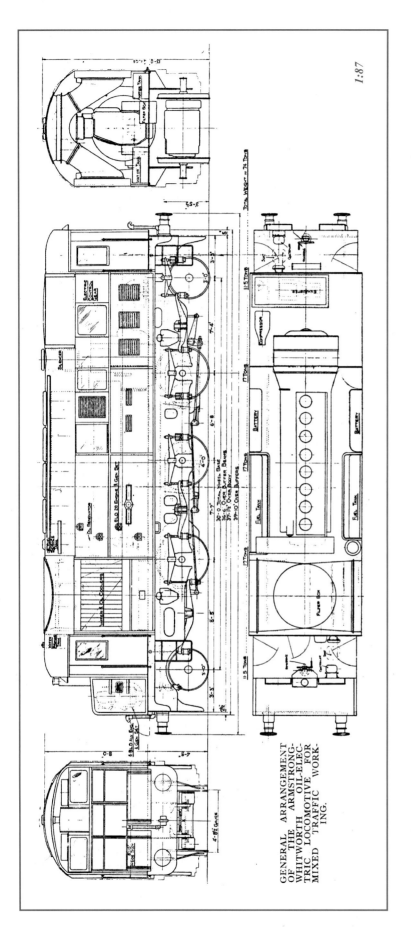

GENERAL ARRANGEMENT OF THE ARMSTRONG WHITWORTH OIL-ELECTRIC LOCOMOTIVE FOR MIXED TRAFFIC WORKING.

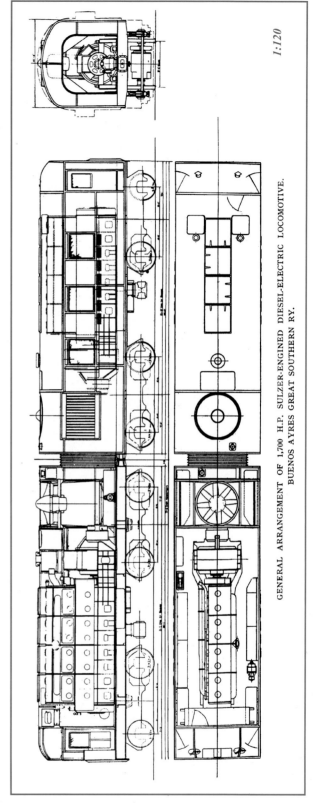

GENERAL ARRANGEMENT OF 1,700 H.P. SULZER-ENGINED DIESEL-ELECTRIC LOCOMOTIVE. BUENOS AYRES GREAT SOUTHERN RY.

Left: The Armstrong Whitworth LNER 1-C-1 of 1933

Above: The Buenos Aires Great Southern Railway 1,700 hp twin-unit locomotive of 1932.

The selection of photos over the next few pages is merely a hint at the variety and quantity of diesels & electrics built for export!

Diesel-electric shunting locomotives based upon the LMS/WD design were built by English Electric and exported throughout the world as well as being supplied to British Railways. In order to suit local conditions variations to the design were made, as seen in these two above photographs of the Federated Malay State Railways class 15 version. This 0-6-0D, no. 151.18, was supplied in 1948 and was still working 35 years later in June 1983 at Gemas depot, also home to some English Electric class 20 Co-Cos. *Photo: Keith R. Chester.*

In this evocative view from mid-1964, Malayan carriage shunter no. 151.08, complete with match truck, comes into Singapore station for the stock of the inbound 'Magic Arrow Express'. When they were introduced in 1948 these locomotives were the first diesels on the FMSR. *Photo: L.A. Summers.*

The North British works were generating overseas orders by the early 1950s and Nigeria received some 3'6" gauge Bo-Bo hood units which were numbered into the class 10 series. No. 1008 had once served as the loco for the Royal train but is seen here in 1961 on more routine duties at Zaria. Similar locomotives were also supplied to other parts of Africa, Sri Lanka, and probably elsewhere. *Photo: Graham Ray.*

The close relationship between Vulcan Foundry and English Electric resulted in fifteen 3000 hp, 3kV DC electrics for the 5'3" gauge Brazilian E.F. Santos - Jundiaí (formerly the São Paulo Ry.). These 110 km/h Co-Cos replaced Garratts on the top express workings after their introduction in 1949. Vulcan works nos. were E32-E46, EE nos. 1779-1793 and EFSJ nos. 1000-1014.

Photo: Harold Cross, courtesy of Brian Orrell.

In 1953 English Electric subcontracted to Vulcan Foundry for the construction of fourteen single-ended A1A-A1A diesel-electrics. They were delivered to the metre gauge Rede Ferrovia de Nordeste (North Eastern Railway) in Brazil for passenger services based around Recife, where no. 704 is preserved. Vulcan works nos. were D195-D207, EE works nos. 2032-2044 and the Brazilian running nos. 701-713.

Photo: Harold Cross, courtesy of Brian Orrell.

English Electric built ten 103-ton 2-Co-Co-2 diesel-electric locos for New Zealand's 3'6" gauge railways in 1954. These 1,500 hp machines, NZR class Df, were typical of the types of locomotives being exported to Commonwealth countries and show obvious similarities to types later adopted by British Railways.

New Zealand Railways publicity photograph.

In 1957, between construction of the first and second batches of Rhodesia Railways 3'6" gauge class DE.2 1-Co-Co-1s, English Electric supplied some basically similar class 20 Co-Cos to Malaya. Having completed its run from Kuala Lumpur to Singapore, no. 20109 'Butang' runs round through the station and goes off to shed passing 0-6-0DE shunter 151.08 taking charge of its stock.
Photo: L.A. Summers.

The British steam era practice of naming locomotives continued into the diesel era with plates on one side of the loco cast in Malaysian script and with Roman characters on the other side. Co-Co diesel electric No. 20114 'Bunga Kala' was seen at Gemas depot in June 1983.
Photo: Keith R. Chester.

The Alco PA type may have been influential in the styling used by English Electric for locos built at the Vulcan Foundry for Egypt and Australia. Although there is a superficial resembance to the 'Deltic', Egypt's locos bore little mechanical similarity. These 1A-Do-A1 machines were said to have evolved more from the LMS pioneer diesels, nos. 10000/10001 and not to have seen further development, particularly as a bogie chassis was clearly a superior arrangement. This illustration is taken from a 1951 Vulcan Foundry advert.

The De Dion Bouton Railcars of the Hedjaz Railway *by Wolfgang Ewers*

In 1928 the De Dion Bouton works, located in Puteux near Paris, constructed four petrol-mechanical railcars and matching trailers. According to one source they were initially delivered to the Tramway Libanais, a 1005 mm gauge line running along the Mediterranean coast northwards from Beirut to Mameltein. The Tramway Libanais was controlled by the DHP (Société Ottomane du Chemin de Fer de Damas - Hama et Prolongements) which by that time not only operated the Beirut - Rayak - Damascus line but also administered the CFH (Chemin de Fer du Hedjaz), the Syrian part of the Hedjaz Railway.

By 1932 the railcars were transferred to the CFH and used to transport railway gangers. With one railcar having been withdrawn from service many years ago the remaining three railcars have been serving the CFH for

De Dion Bouton Railcar ACM 3 standing in front of the locomotive shed at Derra'a.

decades and were to be seen in passenger service on all CFH lines. They were regularly used on the Damascus - Derra'a line as well as on the branch line to Bosra. In the early 1980s they were finally withdrawn from regular service and replaced by Hungarian railcars built by Ganz Mavag in Budapest.

The four De Dion Bouton railcars were numbered ACM 1-4 (A = 1st class; C = 3rd class; M = Motrice, i.e. motor car), whereas the trailers were numbered CR 1 - 4 (C = 3rd class; R = Remorque, i.e. trailer). Upon delivery the railcars had teak bodies and beneath their frame they had a non-powered bogie at the front and an axle powered by a petrol engine via a cardan shaft at the rear. Later the petrol engines were replaced by 110 hp six-cylin-

der diesel engines.

The most interesting feature was their built-in turntable carried underneath. When the railcar reached its destination, it was detached from its trailer. Then two wooden beams were laid across the rails under the railcar. After that the turntable was lowered by a crank on to the beams. A few more revolutions then lifted the railcar clear from the rails, allowing it to be pushed round manually to face the other direction. The railcar was then lowered back onto the rails by reversing the procedure and coupled to its trailer. In their later years this mechanism was not used and the railcars were turned on triangles (located in Bosra and Derra'a).

After first attempts to start the diesel engine of railcar had failed, a PW Department yellow painted Land Rover came to the rescue. Seemingly the lead battery carried on board was powerful enough to get the railcar's engine running. (9th October 2002).

After its recent overhaul at Cadem Works railcar ACM 3 was moved to Derra'a where it was displayed and operated for the participants of the Intraexpress travel group tour on October 9th 2002. As to the trailers, at least one example survived in serviceable condition and was seen in storage outside Cadem Works a day later.

According to the "Livret de la marche des trains" from March 1st 1944, the dimensions were as follows:

	Railcars ACM 1-4	Trailers CR I - 4
Length over buffers (mm)	9,660	5,940
Weight empty (kg)	10,820	4,360
Weight loaded (kg)	13,820	6,360
Maximum speed (kph)	50	50
Number of seats 1st class	8	-
Number of seats 3rd class	20	32

Above: A stunning sight for the kids: teak-bodied railcar ACM 3 on the CFH line between Mesmie and Deiar Ali.

Left: In the driver's compartment of the ACM 3 is the sound insulated engine, a simple dashboard and just visible behind a partition, the driver's seat.

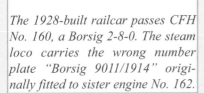

The 1928-built railcar passes CFH No. 160, a Borsig 2-8-0. The steam loco carries the wrong number plate "Borsig 9011/1914" originally fitted to sister engine No. 162.

17

Turning ACM 3 on the built-in turntable. With the front of the railcar carrying the engine, the weight distribution is uneven and several people have to act as a counterbalance at the back to accomplish the procedure.

The built-in turntable under the DeDion Bouton railcar in close-up.

At least one trailer survives at Cadem works in Damascus stored betweena four-wheeled ex-DHP coach (once employed on the Serghaya branch) and the trailer of a Ganz Mavag DMU set.

One of the Mark IV versions of the LEW Bo-Bo electrics at the Fuxin Mining Railway, no. 6607. This loco dates from 1951 and was built for export to the USSR but was donated to China by the Russians around 1953/54, probably in an aid exchange programme or for political reasons.

With the power station cooling towers behind, IV KP1 Mark IIIs 6581 and 6592 work a double-headed train in July 2002, not an everyday sight. Though the IV KP1 is designed for dual control, the connection between the two locomotives was not made in this case and both were in effect operating separately.

With the slope out of Haizhou Pit long and gently graded the IV KP1 Bo-Bo can work on its own to bring trains up out of the pit, as shown by Mark IV no. 6616 at work in May 2001, though the load is restricted to six wagons. 6616 is the only locomotive which has a different works number from its running number, being works no. 6626 of 1951.

Early Narrow Gauge Diesels of Indonesia *by Ray Gardiner*

During my research into industrial railways of Indonesia I came across a list of locomotives at sugar mills in the 1925 Archief voor de Suiker Industie in Netherlands Indies, which was the annual journal for the sugar industry. It came as a surprise to see that some 128 diesel or petrol powered locos were in use this early. There were 180 sugar mills open in 1925, but the list misses details for 8 of them. Almost all of the mills had a rail system, but not all of them had locomotives and would have used animal power. The list also shows some 565 steam locos in use, but there are known to be at least another 19 steam and 2 petrol locos at mills where details are missing.

There was also one battery electric loco delivered just after the list was printed. This was AEG 2960/1925 a 139hp 4wBE centre cab loco built to 1067mm gauge

700mm gauge veteran Oberursel 0-6-0DM, 'LM', at Gempol sugar mill in September 1995.

which was used to shunt the exchange siding at Soekoredjo sugar mill.

Most of the diesel locos were supplied by German builders, mainly Orenstein & Koppel, Deutz aand Oberursel. Another list dated 1930 unfortunately only shows the total number of locos in use and total horsepower, but it appears that many of these diesel locos were out of service by 1930. Most of the diesel locos were less than 30hp, so were much less powereful than most of the steam locos in use. Possibly the diesel locos were found to be unreliable at this early stage and maintenance in Indonesia may have been a problem. From the 1930s many sugar mills were closed and locos were transferred to other mills for further use. Some new steam locos were delivered, but there were no new diesels until the 1950s.

Of these early diesel locos only two are known to have survived. These are the Oberursel 0-6-0DM at Gempol mill which closed in 1995. It is possible that this loco was the 12hp loco at Ardjowinangoen in the 1925 list, going to Gempol which was 6km away after Ardjowinangoen mill closed, both mills being owned by the same company. The other survivor is Rejosari no. 15 'MALABAR' an 0-6-0DM which still sees service, now powered by a Steyer motor. The shedmaster thought that it was built about 1950, however, other people say it dates from the 1920s and there was a 45hp O&K diesel shown in the 1925 list. Unfortunately there is no identification on it.

Apart from sugar mills there were not many early diesel or electric locos used. There were about 27 600mm gauge AEG electric locos built between 1907 and 1925 used at coal mines in Sumatra.

Two Baguley (builder nos. 1383 & 1517) 0-4-0DM built 1924 at Singkep tin mine, builder's no 679 0-4-0DM built 1916 for Anglo Dutch Estates and builder's no. 794 built 1920 for United Serdang Rubber in Sumatra. Another old survivor is builder's no. 3352/1933, a 4wDM now at Kedawung sugar mill, number 21, but it may not have been delivered here.

Baldwin Locomotive Works supplied at least two 0-4-0PM, builder's no. 54743/1920 which went to Mojoppangung sugar mill (700mm), and 54749 which probably went to Kenongo (600mm), both mills being owned by the same company and for which details are not shown in the 1925 list.

Berliet Motor Co in France, better known as a motor car manufacturer, supplied two 600mm gauge 4wPM locos for Sragi mill by 1925

Blackstone & Co Ltd of Stamford UK supplied two 25hp 0-4-0PM locos to the 750mm gauge Banjaratma sugar mill between 1921 and 1925.

Brookville, USA supplied seven 700mm gauge 4wDM locos to the Goodyear Wingfoot Estate, Sumatra between 1927 and 1939, builders nos. 1187, 2111 to 2215 and 2437, and 3 more in 1951, builder nos. 3741 to 3743. Another six 600mm gauge locos went to Sokoramah Sisal near Semerang in 1941, builder nos. 2621 to 2624, 2664 and 2672. Ten 600mm gauge locos went to salt railways at Kaliangat, Madura in 1948, builder nos. 3452 to 3461. Builder nos. 3479 to 3483 were 700mm gauge 4wDM locos shown as going to Government Forestry, Java, but probably went to Assembagus sugar mill. 3479 is Assembagus 6 and was still running in 2002.

Davenport 2284 & 2285 of 1939, 0-4-0DM model DM6, went to Nederlandsche Koloniale Petroleum Maatschappij, Soengoi Gorong, Palembang, Sumatra, shown as 36" gauge.

Deutz built about 60 locos for Indonesia between 1908 and 1938, 29 of which went to sugar mills. Two went to Singkep tin

Rejosari Mill's 700mm gauge 0-6-0 diesel-mechanical no. 15 'Malabar' inside the shed on 2nd August 1997.

mine in 1908 and 1910. At least 22 locos of 600, 700 and 1000mm gauge went to Bataafsche Petrol Mij, Balikpapan, Borneo. The oil refinery was at Balikpapan and was 1000mm gauge, the 600 and 700 mm gauge locos probably going to small oil fields nearby. A number of photos of locos at Balikpapan are on the Australian War Memorial website, www.awm.gov.au

There were two DuCroo & Brauns 5hp 750mm gauge tractors at Colomadu mill in 1924 and builder nos. 15 to 17 built 1924 were 700mm gauge 0-4-0DM to Genietropen KNIL, Surabaya.

Motorail Simplex supplied nine 40hp locos in 1920/21 of which six went to sugar mills. Many more were supplied from 1972, mainly to forestry lines on Kalimanten and Sumatra and palm oil plantations on Sumatra, with a few going to sugar mills.

Ruston Hornsby supplied at least 30 locos to sugar mills, palm

oil plantations on Sumatra and forestry lines at Cepu and Bojonegoro.

There were 39 Orenstein & Koppel and Montania locos shown in the 1924 list, and 21 Oberursel, but as far as I know builders lists do not survive. Several locos were supplied by Knox, Cummings, Duplex, Fordson and Benz, but I have not been able to find out anything about them.

Two 30hp locos are shown as 'Eigan' which means own production in Dutch. They were used at Tjokroetoelong sugar mill which was 700 mm gauge.

Kato built a large number of diesel locos for the Japanese Imperial Navy for use during WWII, at least one being used near Balikpapan, Borneo (AWM website photo 12506).

There were more O&K locos from the 1950s, but the predom-

1925 Archief voor de Suiker Industrie in Netherlands Indies																	
Horsepower	5	6	8	10	12	15	20	25	30	35	40	45	50	60	80	120	**Total**
O&K				3		17	1		12				5	1			39
Deutz						10	6	3	8	1		1					29
Oberursel			1	3	8	5	4										21
Daimler		8	3		1												12
Simplex										1	4	1					6
VIW										2		1					3
Benz.						1									1	1	3
Baldwin										2							2
Blackstone								2									2
Fordson											1	1					2
Berliet								2									2
Duplex											2						2
D&B	2																2
Cummings														1			1
Knox														1			1
Eigan									2								2
Unknown						2											2
Total	2	8	4	6	9	35	11	7	22	9	4	4	5	3	1	1	130
Total hp	10	48	32	60	108	525	220	175	660	315	160	180	250	180	80	120	3108

inant builder was Schoema who built about 320 locos from 1949 and Diema with about 60 locos from 1953. From the 1970s the Japanese builders Hokuriku Juki and Keio supplied many locos.

The main line railways did not start to get diesels until 1953 with the CC200 class Co-Co locos from GE, however, they had electric locos used between Jakarta and Bogor. These locos were from SLM in 1924 and 1927, Borsig/AEG in 1930, Werkspoor 1924, 1925 and 1928 and AEG in 1928.

Any further information anyone can add would be welcomed by the author, contactable at GRaygardiner@aol.com

References:
Archief voor de Suiker Industrie in Nederlands Indies, 1925, pages 279 to 303 - loco list.
Archief voor de Suiker Industrie in Nederlands Indies, 1925, page 653 - AEG loco at Soekoredjo.
DuCroo & Brauns Locomotives, Jan de Bruin.
Eric Fresne information from Foundation Berliet.
Various builders lists. Jens Merte CD ROM www.merte.de
Australian War Memorial, www.awm.gov.au
Baldwin Locomotives Magazine, July 1926.
Davenport and Vulcan Iron Works builders lists from B Lehmuth, USA.
Bill Dickins information and drawing of Blackstone locos.
Locomotive Roster PJKA, Indonesia - Philip Graham.

Indonesian Sugar Plantation Diesels
Photos by Ray Gardiner

1 horse-power and 110 horse-power! 12 ton 0-6-0D no. D3 runs over criss-crossing 700mm gauge tracks at the Pagottan sugar mill in August 1997. This loco was built by Schoema, works number 3120 of 1968.

Shunting a train of loaded cane cars at Purwodadi mill is 6WDM no. 1. Schoema also built this machine (1290/1951), a 13 ton loco rated at 90 hp.

Brookville 0-4-0D no. 6 dates from the late 1950s and was seen working in the yard at Assembagus on 19th August 1999.

Another Assembagus engine, 0-4-0D no. 13, pictured in 1997. No builder's plate was carried but other locos of the same design were seen carrying two plates - Ebara, Tokyo and Hokuriku Juki, Tokyo.

4WDM no. 10 on the 600mm gauge system at Soedhono Mill, manufactured by Diema in 1951, works no. 1676, and pictured on 31st July 1997.

600mm gauge Moës 0-4-0D at Pangka, July 1997. The loco carries fine mesh grilles on the sides of the engine compartment, barely discernable in the picture.

Tasikmadu Mill's system is of 750 mm gauge and employs 1951 vintage Ruston Hornsby 0-4-0D no. TM.D.1 (maker's no. 285961). Note the double roof for cab ventilation in the tropical heat.

Orenstein & Koppel supplied numerous diesels to Java's mills, including 0-4-0D no. 01 on the 700mm gauge Mojopang-gung system, works no. 25576, pictured on 11th August 1996.

An obviously well used 750mm gauge Orenstein & Koppel 0-4-0D at Ceper Mill, O&K no. 26567, 1st August 1997.

Back in July 1989 a 700mm gauge O&K jackshaft drive 0-6-0D was bringing in the cane at Rejoagung, loco no. 1A in the mill's fleet, O&K works no. 25625.

Another O&K jackshaft drive loco built for the same gauge as the one above but to a slightly different design. This example was working cane trains at Kebonagung in August 1997, numbered C5, builder's number not known.

Diesels and Electrics of Cuba *by Peter Smith*

INTRODUCTION

Readers of Locomotives International magazine will be aware (from issues 13,16 & 27) that the first steam locomotives in Cuba were British, but the USA quickly gained the ascendancy and was the major supplier for the remainder of the steam era. In the case of Cuba the end of new steam acquisitions came relatively early (the latest purchases I can find were in 1942 for the steel industry). This is ironic in the light of the subsequent longevity of steam power.

It was therefore perhaps inevitable that the first "main line" diesel acquisitions would be from the USA with mainly "export" type locomotives from General Electric and General Motors (EMD). There were also early purchases from Alco and Baldwin. These were mainly switching locomotives and as early as 1925 Cuba was bringing in small switchers and railcars from the above firms and also from the smaller American builders such as Whitcomb and Brookville. US electric locomotives and railcars were brought in for the Hershey Railway in 1920.

PURCHASES FROM EUROPE

As in the case of steam there were only isolated purchases from Europe up to the time of the revolution in 1959.

MAK 0-8-0 Diesel Hydraulics

Between 1955 and 1957 FC Occidentales purchased 61 large 0-8-0 diesel hydraulics from MAK in three batches with successively more powerful engines. One of these is believed to have been named after General Batista, the President, but I cannot recollect where I saw a photograph. So far as is known all have been scrapped. This can never be an absolute conclusion in Cuba however, as since the revolution the demarcation between the main line (F de C, now FC), the sugar mills and other large indus-

tries such as ports, steel and cement has been blurred. A number of ex-main line diesels have migrated to these industries and discoveries continue to occur.

Brissoneau and Lodz Bo-Bo Diesel-Electrics

13 Sulzer powered DEs were purchased by FC Occidentales in 1954/55. All are believed to have been scrapped except for one which was the subject of a one-off conversion to overhead electric for the 1200V Hershey system and numbered 21202 (see photo).

THE IMPACT OF THE REVOLUTION

After the revolution the dominance of the USA was ultimately replaced by domination by the USSR. After a quiet start the 1970s became the era of the "Alcoski" - Russian locomotives built to essentially Alco designs. Purchases from mainland Europe were mainly from Russia but despite the US embargo, windows of opportunity for other European imports did arise.

United Kingdom

Hunslet 204 hp DM

At least two (possibly three) 204hp diesel mechanicals were supplied by Hunslet in 1960. These are the only known locomotives in the 40000 series (see LI 27). 40201 was noted by usually reliable sources at Granma sugar mill as late as 1997 and 40203 in Havana in 1983.

Brush

In 1965/66 Brush supplied (via Clayton) 10 class 47 looka-likes (52501-10). These reportedly had a short working life and after a long period in storage (LI 27) all were scrapped at Cardenas in the late 1990s. The story of these locomotives and the

Brissoneau & Lodz Bo-Bo diesel-electric number 21202, pictured in February 2002, converted to 1200V overhead electric for service on the 'Hershey' system in Cuba.

26

Brush Class S1 Bo-Bo diesel-electric no. 2726 at work with a long loaded cane train on the Hermanos Ameijeiras system in April 2002.

S1s described below is covered in George Toms book 'Brush Locomotives 1940-78' (TPC/Turntable Publications).

In 1968/9 Brush supplied 15 class S1 Bo-Bo DEs of 3 foot gauge for sugar mill use. A number of these survive at Hermanos Ameijeiras sugar mill having given good service for over 30 years.

Czechoslovakia

20 Ceskomoravska-Kolben-Danek, (Prague) class T458.0 Bo-Bo DEs were supplied in 1964. These, numbered 50701-20, seem to be coming to the end of their lives.

France

Around 30 Brissoneau and Lodz M60 DEs (50801-30) similar to the pre-revolution 60800 series locomotives were purchased in 1965. It is not known whether any survive in main line service, most having disappeared in the 1980s, but one was noted in Havana in 2000 and another in that year in cement industry use (Artemisa).

Hungary

A large number of Ganz Mavag class DVM9 Bo-Be DEs in the 61000 series were purchased in 1969. These are being cannibalised or scrapped and it is not known whether any remain in service.

It would be remiss not to mention the 1975/76 purchases of MX624 locos from Fiat Concorde (South America) and Bombardier (Canada). These Alco derivatives have been the mainstay of Cuban motive power recently. Most recently second-hand US-designed locomotives have arrived from Canada and Mexico.

ČKD Class T458.0 No 50707 at Camaguey works, Cuba in February 2002

"HOMEBUILT" DIESEL LOCOMOTIVES

The privations of the US embargo have caused severe motive power shortages throughout the post-revolution era. This has, as well as extending the steam era in the sugar industry, caused the exercise of much ingenuity to produce diesel locomotives for switching and maintenance of way duties in the sugar mills. These include steam locomotive conversions and a variety of other homebuilts. Rather less than 20 steam locomotive conversions have been recorded, covering standard and narrow gauge. Most are 0-4-0s or 2-4-0s with a few 2-6-0s. Some others are not steam loco conversions but have steam loco cabs. In most cases Russian tractor engines are used but Mercedes engines are becoming available for re-powering projects.

Steam-diesel conversion no. 1420 at Australia Sugar Mill, Cuba, in March 2000, used mainly on permanent way duties. Originally this was a 2-4-2ST, Baldwin builder's no. 42346.

Steam-to-diesel loco conversion no. 4136 at Espartaco Sugar Mill Cuba, April 2002. (Some doubt the steam heritage of this loco).

Steam-diesel conversion no. 0007 (numbered '5' on the front of the hood) at G.A. Mañalich Sugar Mill, April 2002. The original steam locomotive from which this creation arose was a Manning Wardle 0-6-0ST built in 1873. The boiler/firebox/smokebox was still present in 2002.

Cuban 3'0" gauge 'homebuilt' locomotive no. 1979 stored in the shed at the Parque Lenin in February 2002.

'Homebuilt' Bo-Bo diesel No 4163 at Primero de Mayo Sugar Mill, February 2002. Note the diesel or electric trucks and the re-used steam locomotive cab.

Another Cuban 'homebuilt' four-wheel diesel, this one was found at the Antonio Sanchez Sugar Mill in April 2002, also with a steam locomotive's cab.

Railbuses and Railcars

Cuba has many railbuses and railcars. Some are American survivors or more recent US acquisitions via Canada. Many are homebuilt using kits of parts from Hungary and South America (resulting from European initiatives e.g. Fiat in Argentina). Others are from Europe, including the electric railcars from Spain (Barcelona) now the main-stay of Hershey passenger services and the recent acqui-sition of ex-DB "Ferkeltaxi" diesel railcars and trailers.

Cuban Railbus 4140 at Las Tunas February 2002. Made from parts supplied from Hungary.

Cuban Fiat (Argentina) railbus no. 2147 at Havana CA Coubre Station in February 2002.

Right: FC Cuba (Hershey Railway) electric train led by car 405 at Casablanca (Havana) Station in March 2000. This is one of the railcar sets formerly employed in Spain by the F.C. Generalidad de Catalunya.

Please note: The foregoing is not intended to be definitive but is simply the result of observation and some research. I would be pleased to learn of errors and omissions and the editor would be glad to publish further details.

What is All This About Three-Phase Locomotives? *by P.M. Kalla-Bishop*

This previously unpublished article was originally written by the late P.M. Kalla-Bishop in 1991.

A new type of motive power is taking over on the railway scene, loosely referred to by British engineers as three-phase. It is suggested that this is a misnomer, the result of lack of training in a fresh technology and a neglect of railway history. The three-phase traction motors used have been seized upon as the first recognisable item. As noted below the innovation and heart of the new motive power is a solid-state current inverter. Therefore current inverter locomotives and emus would appear to be the right name.

Three-phase electric current was the original preferred method of main line electrification, albeit it involved a pair of separately insulated contact wires above the track (the earthed rails made up the third phase) and the locomotives had only four fixed running speeds. Apart from a line in Switzerland in 1899, it appeared in Italy in 1901 on trial. Eventually Italy had 1,363 route miles of the electrification and there were a few short railways elsewhere, one or two of which still survive. In Italy three-phase has been eliminated in favour of 3,000 V dc, the last route operating in 1976.

The 1901 Italian trial branch line was equipped by Ganz & Co of Budapest and by their young engineer Kálmán Kandó (1869-1931). He and his team spent most of the next 14 years in Italy, and Kandó is one of the world's great names in railway electrification. From 1914 Kálmán Kandó turned his mind to single phase, 50 Hz, ac electrification. A trial locomotive ran successfully at Budapest in the 1920s and the Budapest - Hegyshalom route (the latter on the Austrian border)

was electrified on the Kandó system 1932-1934. This 50 Hz, overhead catenary gave the Hungarians a flying start when the conventional 25 KV, 50 Hz, electric locomotive appeared upon the scene.

What the 1-D-1 Kandó locomotives did with their single phase 50 Hz power supply need not detain us, except to remark that a single large three-phase or more traction motor was fitted. This drove the wheels through cranks and coupling rods, and could provide four fixed running speeds only. At this point the reader may care to be reminded that alternating current (ac) flows first in one direction and then the other. Each cycle to and fro occurs so many times per second, a figure termed the frequency

Above: Kandó 1-D-1 no. V40.016 was built by MAVAG with Ganz electrical equipment in 1934 for work on the Budapest - Hegyeshalom line, electrified at 16 kV 50Hz. Twenty-nine such locomotives were built, this last remaining example now being displayed at the Museum Park in Budapest following restoration by Ganz.   Photo: Paul Catchpole.

Left: an example of the Hungarian class V55 three-phase Co-Co electric, no. V55.004, now withdrawn and preserved at Budapest's railway museum. Photo: Paul Catchpole.

and measured in hertz (Hz). In Europe electricity is generated for industrial and domestic use at 50Hz, hence the attraction of 50 Hz railway electrification. It is also why electric clocks keep time incidentally. An important characteristic of the three-phase electric motor is that it revolves at a rate determined by the frequency of the ac supplied, a lower frequency and it slows down, a higher and it speeds up.

Nearly 100 years ago it was realised that locomotives with three-phase traction motors supplied at varying frequencies could be used to run trains. How to do it was the question. Attempts have been made, the Hungarian State with its V44 and V55 classes of 1944 and 1950 and the French National with its

The Italian State Railways diesel-alternator current inverter Bo-Bo Class D145 designed for hump shunting, trip working and branch line duties. They are fitted with two 700 hp engines, one or other of which can be closed down completely when performing light duties. Photo: Fiat Savigliano SpA.

CC14000 class of 1954. These locomotives ran all right, but they were costly and not a little clumsy in operation as they were electro-mechanical machines. These classes have been withdrawn from traffic. Then in the United States two firms simultaneously invented the solid-state thyristor in 1953.

The thyristor can be thought of as a solid-state electric switch, either on or off. It can be arranged also to switch dc, first to flow in one direction then in the other direction. Should this switching be fast enough the output will be alternating current. Thus dc is inverted to ac. The switching rate (frequency) can be adjusted readily by altering the value of the weak reference current, say by an engine drive, to alter the speed of the traction motors. Three banks of these switches (one for each phase) to a quantity suitable for the duty are provided. There remains a difficulty of getting the locomotive to start, the motors calling for low voltage and a high current. This is done by setting the inverter to a low frequency and frequency modulating the result for the desired high current. Everyone knows about frequency modulation (FM) disc jokeys are everlastingly gabbling about it to give notice they are transmitting on 95.8 MHz FM or whatever. A pulse wave goes on until the locomotive is moving at little over walking pace. Then the inverter takes over its near lowest frequency.

Brush of Loughborough tried out current inverter locomotive 'Hawk' in 1965 (the locomotive was former BR prototype diesel 10800). This was a failure, probably the aspiration outran the technology of the day. Then Brown Boveri of Mannheim put in five years development on a traction current inverter. The firm is now part of Asea-Brown Boveri (ABB). Fitted to a new Co-Co diesel in 1971 (later DM 202.002-2) this was a great success. A Swiss Federal motor van was rebuilt to straight electric current inverter Be 4/4 12001 in 1972. The DB locomotive was coupled to a motor coach to provide a pantograph and transformer, and ran as a straight electric also for a time. The first commercial order

came in 1975, a batch of Co-Co hump and trip-working locomotives for the Swiss Federal Basle yards. The current inverter locomotive was on its way.

Whenever necessary the incoming current to a current inverter locomotive is taken through two preliminary stages. First a transformer to cut the voltage, and then a solid-state rectifier to produce dc. The dc is held at a constant voltage for presentation to the inverter by chopper circuits. The chopper interrupts the traction current and delivers it in bursts, short bursts for low voltage and longer for higher voltage, with proportionate changes in the current value. The current inverter under the control of the driver delivers the frequency, voltage and current values necessary to work the train. The above is based on ABB practice, but other inverter manufacturers often have different circuitry ideas. Thus the choppers mentioned above are reinforced by Siemens and used for voltage and current control, the inverter merely looking after frequency. The French have had even more drastic ideas, although at the moment they seem likely to abandon them in future. Diesel current inverter locomotives are not very different, save that a transformer is not needed and that the normal control of engine revolutions is used to aid the inverter in the supply of the required voltage and current.

Simple explanations of complex entities are always difficult, and above all that has been attempted is an outline of the main principle used by current inverter locomotives. Necessary adjunct circuitry has been omitted, and other matters glided across. It might be noted that as all locomotives' traction current is converted to dc aboard, the design of multi-supply locomotives is simplified. A limitation to this is that 750 V and 1,500 V dc supplies often cannot deliver sufficient current to take advantage of a locomotive's full potential output at higher voltages. Unless drivers keep a sharp eye on the ammeter, bits of British Rail's Southern Region may be yet brought to a halt by the proposed

Class 465, let alone by TGVs, as sub-station overcurrent relays drop out.

Locomotives drawing single phase ac can be equipped with a controlled rectifier to supply steady voltage in the dc link, as on the DB's Class 120 of 1979. When in the regenerative braking mode, the ac generated by the ac traction motors flows through current inverter to feed the dc link. Importantly, a four-quadrant controller in the rectifier can invert this dc feed into single phase ac to pass back into the overhead catenary system.

A recent innovation has been the gate turn-off thyristor (GTO). It offers more precise switching and it can run at a higher temperature, so fewer expensive thyristors are needed. The heat generated must be dispersed, so at least for higher power current inverters a refrigerant circuit must be fitted. The first European traction GTO thyristors were applied by ABB to a Sihltal, Zurich, Uetliburg Railway Bo-Bo at the end of 1987, closely followed by prototype Milan Metropolitan emus with Mitsubishi GTO inverters in early 1988. The batch of DB Class 120 now being delivered will be known as Class 121 as GTO traction thyristors are fitted, and such fitting is becoming the normal thing.

The current inverter locomotive is fast becoming the standard practice for almost every short of duty. The type is in competition with orthodox chopper and thyristor locomotive types; examples of the latter category are British Rail's Classes 90 and 91. In the end relative costs will decide the issue, although comparisons are not easy. The current inverter unit admittedly has a higher first capital cost, but it is claimed that maintenance and running costs are so low that at the end of a 30 year life the units will be showing a good profit. The oldest current inverter type is barely fifteen years old, but it is bearing out this production unit forecast.

In the spring of 1991 there are some 2,000 current inverter motive power units in traffic in the world. About half of these are Japanese emu dc motor coaches, for from a start in 1984 the Japanese have been building these in quantity to a number of different designs. Most of the rest are running in Europe. The United States has made a start in current inverter adoption, but so far has imported all its current inverters from Europe in default of native production. Meanwhile the pioneer diesel current inverter locomotive of 1971 was passed into the care of the Berlin Transport Museum in 1988.

Italian Three-Phase Electrics *from the camera and collection of Mario Forni*

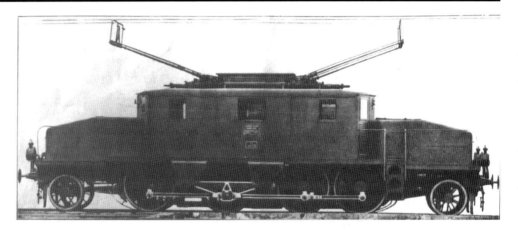

"The most modern and powerful electric locomotive of the Italian State Railways, built by Tecnomasio Italiano Brown Boveri...", from a 1920s advert.

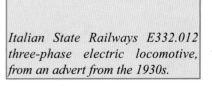

Italian State Railways E332.012 three-phase electric locomotive, from an advert from the 1930s.

An E360 class 3-phase electric locomotive near the entrance to the international Simplon tunnel at Iselle, Italy.
The Simplon tunnel, from Iselle in Italy
to Brigue, Switzerland, was electrified
with the 3.6 kV 16.7 Hz three-phase
system when it was opened in 1906.
(From a postcard, collection
of Giovanni Muzio).

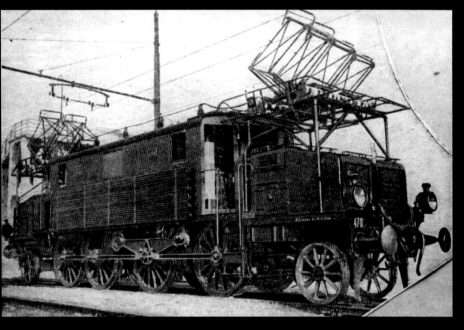

The E470 class locomotives were built in
1928 by T.I.B.B. for the 10kV 43 Hz AC line
running east from Rome to Avezzano and
Sulmana. Much of this industrial frequency
electrification equipment and many of the
locomotives were destroyed during the
Second World War. (Author's collection).

Between 1964 and 1973 Savona
Letimbro station was divided into two
electric systems: 3kV DC and 3.6kV
three-phase AC. In this photograph of
the Torino - Ventimiglia 'Diretto',
taken on 24th July 1971, the two locomotives entering the station have
lowered their pantographs to pass into
the "foreign" section. They are then
detached and shunted back under the
3-phase wires by a diesel shunter or
pushed back by a DC electric locomotive.

Is it a steam engine?! No, it's Italian electric no. E432.018 at Acqui Terme station on 11th July 1975. The resistence banks for the three-phase traction motors were suspended in a tank. Water was pumped into the tank and short-circuited the resistance banks one by one to allow the locomotive to accelerate. The water was also used for resistance cooling and tended to evaporate.

FS 10-wheel, rod-coupled electric loco no. E554.072 works a goods train on the Alessandria - San Giuseppe line on 15th May 1976.

Control trailer Lebc 840.206 and motor coach ALe 840.026 work a local train from Acqui Terme to Asti on 26th March 1976. Lebc 840 class control trailers were equipped with 3-phase pantographs while beneath the floor there were small transformers and rectifiers. Thus equipped, the control trailers could supply the Ale 840 class motor coaches (3kV DC E.M.U.s) with power at their normal 3kV DC.

Direct Drive on Diesel Locomotives *by Gottfried Wild*

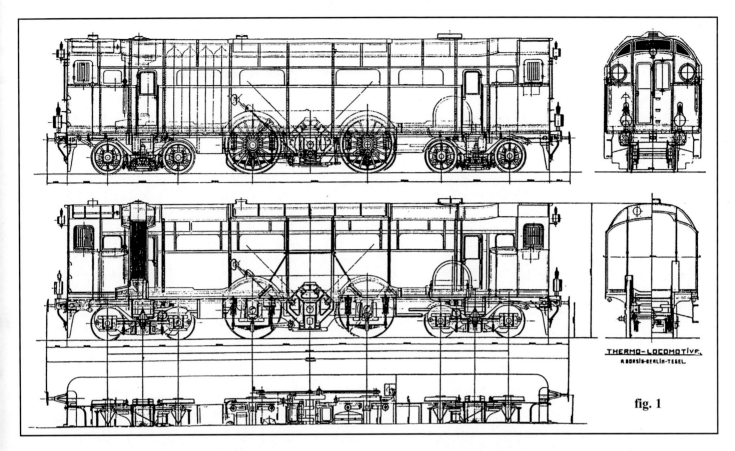

fig. 1

Some readers may remember, the December 1994 issue of the Locomotives International magazine (no. 26) had featured in an article some attempts made to find and develop a suitable power drive in the early days of diesel locomotive construction. A special interest was paid in that dissertation to the compressed air drive. Since my article was published, I've noticed that another earlier and no less important device had been mentioned in fact, but quite neglected since: the direct power drive.

According to some mention in the previous article, the 1912 experimental express locomotive built for the Royal Prussian State Railways by the Borsig Works and Klose Engineering Consortium of Berlin was a joint venture with the Sulzer Works of Winterthur, (fig. 1). It was the first large internal combus-

tion locomotive for main line operation in Europe. Naturally its constructors also hoped that it would become more than an experiment. The materialisation of its design, the test runs and in the end, its failure, have already been described so I will complete that description with some supplementary technical details only.

What is direct drive and how does it work? The internal combustion engine translates the thermal energy developed in a cylinder to crank axle where this power output is transformed into rotations. Coupling rods connected to this crank axle transmit motion to the driving wheels. Both the admirer and connoisseur of today's diesel locomotives, well acquainted with the elegance of hydraulic and electric drives will probably ask, why such a rigid and uncomfortable system? This system is simple indeed! No intermediate gear or other kind of transmission is connected between the motor and driving wheels. That means no supplementary weight, no losses in gears, transmissions and couplings and that also means fuel economies.

At the beginning of the 20th Century the thermal engine had

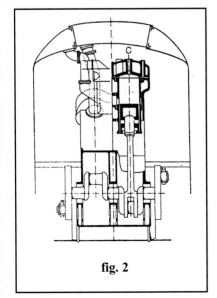

fig. 2

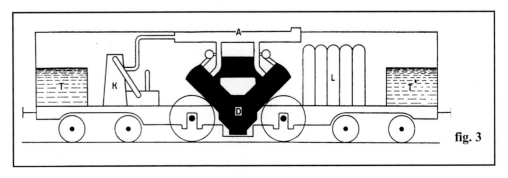

fig. 3

reached a maturity that made it capable of use for rail operation, especially with regard to its sizes and output, both related to the specific weight. Unfortunately, compared to the steam engine, the internal combustion motor has a low torque output at low rotations of the crank axle, furthermore, a minimum speed was required to allow rotation. An intermediate mechanism is required, which should allow no-load operation, high power torque output at low speeds, reversibility and uncomplicated controlling. The electric transmission was considered well suited as an intermediate aggregate between the motor and wheels, allowing a fine and smooth regulation of power output at low speeds too. The main disadvantage of electric drives in those days was the relatively high weight of the dynamo and traction motors, resulting in a disadvantageous power:weight ratio. The Heilmann steam locomotive with electric drive had demonstrated this disadvantage, in spite of satisfactory operation.

Hydraulic transmissions, which are generally smaller sized than electric, were at best a theoretical solution in the first decade of the 20th Century when considered for railway traffic. Interestingly, direct drive was studied and experimented with mostly in Germany and Russia. Except for a further French experiment and some British reflections from 1925, the author has no further information about similar experiments in Europe or America.

The Borsig-Klose-Sulzer locomotive naturally followed the direct drive principle. For the power plant, a 4-cylinder 2-stroke 1000 hp Vee motor was specially developed for this project (fig. 2). The motor was reversible, allowing loco-

motive operation in both directions. Fig. 3 shows the drive system arrangement in this locomotive. Special attention was paid to the smooth running of the complete system as shown in the balancing diagram (fig. 4).

Starting the motor, and at the same time the locomotive, was performed with the help of compressed air kept in steel tanks on the locomotive. To start, the air was let into the motor cylinders, the pressure worked upon the pistons and the locomotive started moving. At a speed of 10 km/h fuel had to be injected into the cylinders and ignition followed immediately, activated by spark plugs. An air compressor fixed on the loco frame, driven by an auxiliary diesel engine refilled the air tanks (fig. 5).

Practical tests soon showed that the "ignition speed" lay higher than expected, causing considerable air consumption, so the air tanks were generally empty before ignition could take place. As a result, the locomotive was often lying powerless on the track in the middle of the landscape waiting for the auxiliary diesel engine to refill the air tanks. Furthermore, the motor's water cooling system was too small.

After several rebuilds, the locomotive was able to continue test runs in Switzerland, its birthplace. This time it proved rela-

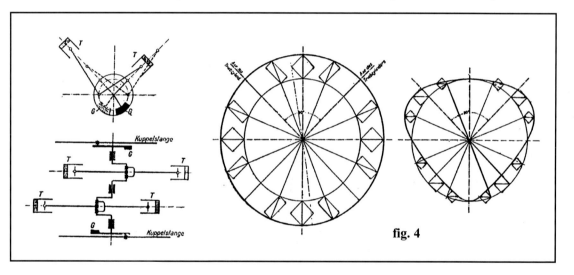

fig. 4

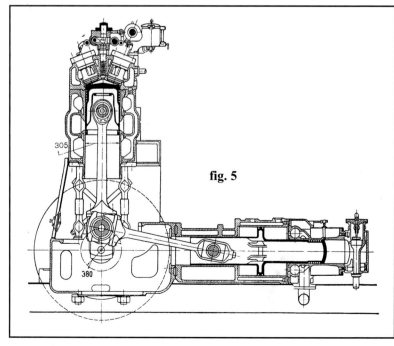

fig. 5

tively reliable, the main weakness, as before, being the compressed air starting. The locomotive had never worked as well as expected. It was as late as 1913 that the locomotive moved under its own power from Winterthur to Berlin. Before new tests could really start the crank axle broke. After a repair was made tests started again but a short time later a cylinder was seriously damaged. The outbreak of World War 1 put a stop to any intention of rebuilding, the locomotive was scrapped and the project abandoned.

The same conflagration had unfortunately stopped and in the end destroyed another similar experiment, the Leroux railcar, (fig. 6). The French Établissements Fives-Lille built in 1913 this eight-wheel railcar for the Société Mines de Carvin. The principle was identical to the Klose locomotive except for the motor, which for reasons of space on such a vehicle, was designed with four opposed pistons running inside two cylinders, one against the other, (fig. 7). Compressor supercharging was used for that motor. Starting was also made with

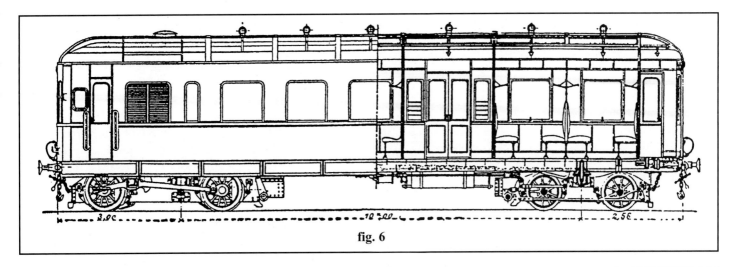

fig. 6

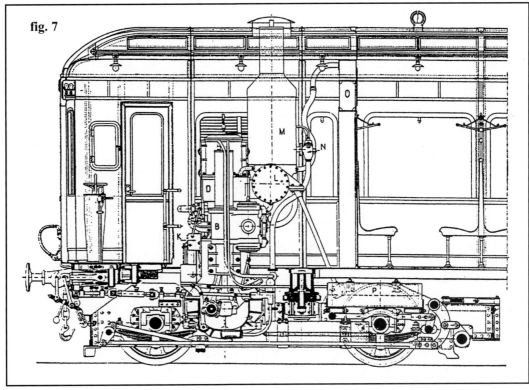

fig. 7

compressed air, as for the German prototype. The 150 hp engine drove via crank axle coupling rods on one bogie's wheels. Only one year later this quite modern looking railcar was destroyed during war operations.

The Klose locomotive was dead but the idea of direct drive survived as much as the Klose Company itself. As it seems, German locomotive builders in particular were fascinated by the simplicity of the direct drive system. Quite uncomplicated indeed, but sometimes a little premature for the technology of those days. Real success would follow some decades later.

A few years further on, in 1919, the Klose Engineering Company in Berlin worked out another similar project. This new large 4-6-4 express locomotive should have had direct drive again (fig. 8) and was designed to develop an output of 800 hp. This time power was divided over 8 cylinders, working on two oscillating crank axles with power being transmitted from these axles to the driving wheels via coupling rods.

It seems obvious to note the tendency to divide the whole power from the motor over more than one crank axle, say to reduce the individual stress per unit and to avoid damage in the bearings and articulations. On the other hand, so many articulations would have produced a real symphony of vibrations and the result could have together eventually produced damaged axles and bearings, as in the first Borsig-Klose experiment. The builders recognised this danger quite soon and the project never came to fruition. No details about the locomotive starting device are available but a supplementary group of four cylinders, easily recognised in the mentioned diagram of this 1919 project, makes a likely supposition that compressed air was again intended for

starting purposes.

Soon after the failure of the Borsig-Klose experiment, the idea of using another kind of a secondary power circuit instead of air and able to proved the energy requested for starting the loco was developed further. As it seems, the choice was not very complicated at all! Steam was still the absolute power on tracks at that time, early in the twenties. The solution was easily found as an amalgamation of both systems: a classical steam locomotive was provided with an auxiliary internal combustion engine, both systems acting on the same set of driving wheels. The unfulfilled projects initiated by Buchli, Switzerland (fig. 9) and by Maschinenfabrik Esslingen in Germany (fig. 10), illustrate such kind of hybrid locomotives. At starting the locomotive would have worked as a pure steam locomotive. After "ignition speed" was reached, fuel would be injected into the diesel cylinders, the steam circuit switched off and the system would work on as an internal combustion engine only.

I consider the Swiss design in fig. 9 is quite remarkable. The diagram features a locomotive with eight cylinders, the outer four ones for steam operation, the others inside the frames for steam operation. Presumably on hard working sections en route, a mixed operation of the locomotive was intended, as the boiler could be kept continuously under pressure by the hot diesel exhaust gases when passing through the smoke pipes of the oil fired boiler on their way to the atmosphere. That means the steam part would have worked as booster too, not only as a starter. The Esslingen project followed a very similar principle. Unfortunately, none of these interesting projects went beyond the stage of a proposal.

Reflecting upon the direct drive diesel locomotive the problem of its starting continued to be the greatest. A further problem was its quite hard and rough working, as explosive ignition inside the combustion engine was transmitted as shocks and vibrations directly to the wheels and to the track. It was also recognised that a coupling device enable the temporary power interruption from the motor to the driving wheels would become a necessity, should the locomotive work satisfactorily.

Russian locomotive builders were also very interested in the development of diesel traction, right from the beginning of the 20th Century. On the Caucasian railway system in particular, poor water quality and the difficulties and cost of its supply for steam locomotives was a serious challenge affecting normal railway operation. The Russians assimilated the direct drive, adding

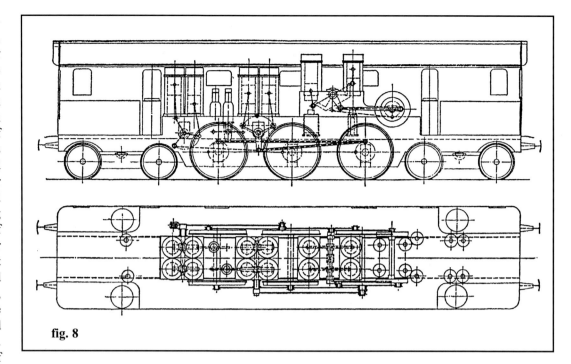

fig. 8

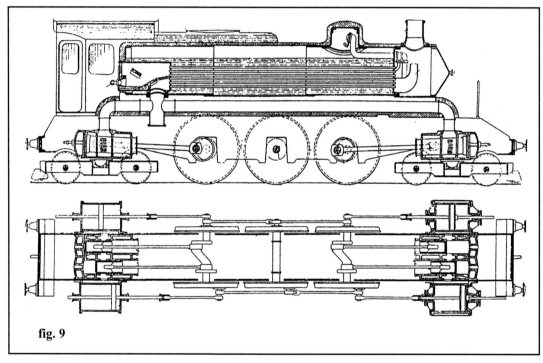

fig. 9

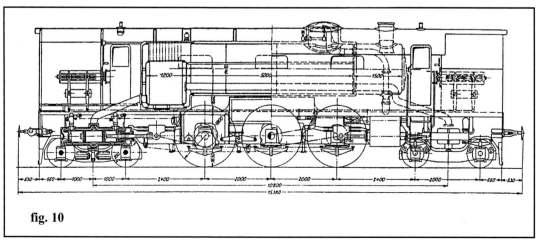

fig. 10

some original proposals around the search for starting devices. Strangely, they produced a large number of remarkable projects, none of them materialising until they really put their creativity into practice at the end of the 1930s, but by then it was destined to be the swansong of the direct drive!

In those early days of the 1900s Grinevetzky and later on his pupil Shelest, both from the Technical University of Moscow, were pioneers in Russian diesel motor design, while Hackel turned his attention to designing diesel locomotives. Jadoff, Prigorsky and Khlebnikoff are three more noteable men to be mentioned in the gallery of Russian diesel locomotive development. The Russian diesel locomotive, however, is most strongly linked to Georgy Vladimir Lomonossoff. After graduating from the Tsarist Institution of Transport in St. Petersburg he at first focused his attention and work upon the steam locomotive. Two years later he moved to Kiev, teaching Railway Technology at the University, coming into contact with Alfons Lipetz and they very soon became good friends. Their Saturday evening debates and studies around railway electrification and dieselisation are legendary in Russian railway history. It may be considered that Lomonossoff continued the work of Rudolf Diesel, both men's lifetime work being of crucial influence upon the development of diesel locomotives in Europe. It is said that Rudolf Diesel, a short time before his tragic and mysterious death on the sea voyage to Great Britain, had designed several types of large locomotive to be powered by his motor. Unfortunately these diagrams are lost and today we may speculate as to whether he had used direct drive on his designs too.

In the years closely following the Bolshevist Revolution Professor Lomonossoff was delegated by the Soviet government to supervise the construction of a large order of 0-10-0 steam locomotives at German factories. In Southern Germany, at Esslingen, where mechanical engineers like Dr. Max Mayer were fascinated by the internal combustion locomotive drive and in the neighbourhood of the Swiss locomotive industry, where the Sulzer Works were pioneers of the new traction technology, Lomonossoff certainly found a most creative entourage. No wonder that as soon as the steam order was fulfilled he continued his experiments in Germany and invested an impressive energy and temperament (legends say he threw his pocket watch on the ground when not satisfied with the results on the test bed!), amalgamated with very unconventional methods, into diesel locomotive studies and projects. Germany at that time offered favourable conditions for research into new technologies. As a result both of war reparation debts to the Entente, and a policy instigated by the newly founded Reichsbahn administration, traditional factories involved in locomotive and motor construction like MAN, Deutz, Esslingen and others were forced to study and develop alternative drives. From Esslingen, where contacts with a fervent promoter of the direct drive, Dr. Mayer, had influenced him, Lomonossoff moved to Hohenzollern AG of Düsseldorf. There, an order from Soviet Russia for a large 1Eo1 diesel electric locomotive was just under construction and Lomonossoff continued his work as technical representative.

Just a few years earlier in 1913, Lomonossoff, when CME of the Tashkent Railways projected a large 2-10-2 freight locomotive with two four-cylinder diesel engines each placed at opposite ends of the locomotive, fig. 11. The motor crank axles were at the same time the jackshafts, being coupled to the wheels by connecting rods. For this project, and this is the novelty, the driving wheels were free running on the axles. Alfons Lipetz, locomotive designer at the same company, designed for this project a compressed air system to enable control of friction couplings placed on the locomotive axles, connecting them to the wheels, fig. 12. The motors were started when the couplings were switched off; after starting, they were switched on and the locomotive was able to get moving. The outbreak of WW1 halted activities in this direction again but the direct drive was not forgotten!

In 1925, another Russian locomotive constructor, Mr. Sidoroff proposed an impressive 4-8-4 passenger locomotive, again using compressed air for starting, stored in a large pressurised air tank almost the size of a steam loco boiler (fig. 13). Two steam locomotive cylinders at the rear end of the vehicle, probably fitted with Walschaert valve gears, worked on the driving wheels. The diesel engine was located beneath the air tank, over the running gear. Six pistons worked in opposition to each other, "head to head", inside 3 horizontal cylinders. A system of driving rods and jackshafts transmitted power to the wheels. The main jackshaft between the central drivers was provided with a friction coupling. At starting the coupling was switched off. Again, nothing more than another project.

We have now looked at several designs and proposals for locomotives with diesel engine propulsion and direct drive.

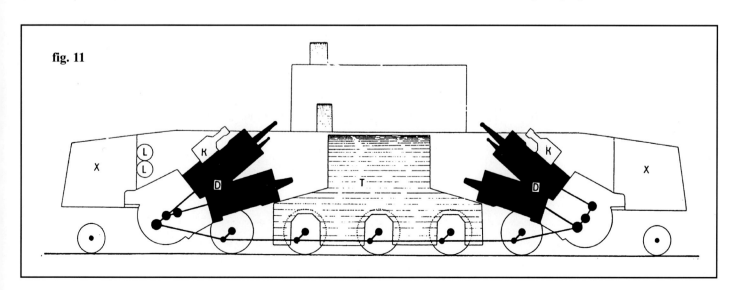

fig. 11

Someone could say those projects were an endless chain of failures, never coming out of the status of a might have been. It's true, some of them were very complicated, others maybe a utopian ideal. Their designs all showed an unmistakable relationship to the steam locomotive, following more or less its principle of power transmission. We must also take into consideration that internal combustion motor technology in the first two decades of the 20th century, was passing from infancy through its childhood age. The principle of direct drive was theoretically very efficient, estimates having figured values up to 30% for such a diesel locomotive. Indeed an impressive result in those days!

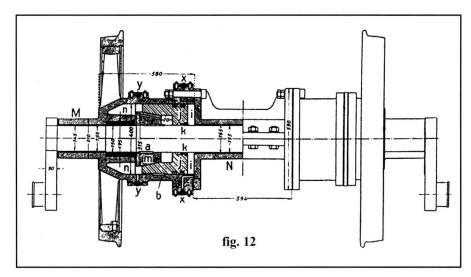

fig. 12

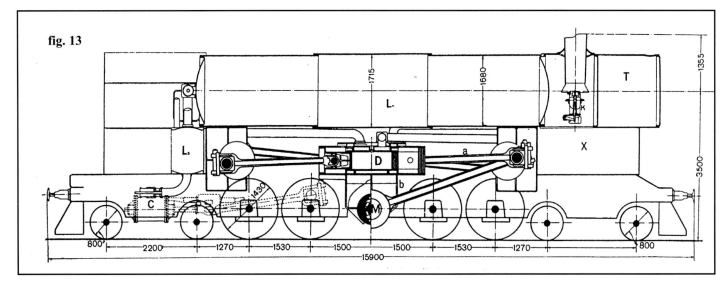

fig. 13

In 1919 the Giovanni Ansaldo Works of Genoa, Italy started intensive research into diesel locomotives and several systems of power drives. In the end, direct power drive was chosen again. In 1928 the efforts came to fruition as a large 2-6-4 experimental loco was outshopped and presented to the Italian State Railways,

(fig. 14). The reader will recognise an already well known working principle; a steam locomotive running gear having two outside cylinders and Walschaerts gear which supported a sandwich of a six cylinder Junkers diesel engine, a locomotive divided upon two levels. Single acting, head to head configured pistons

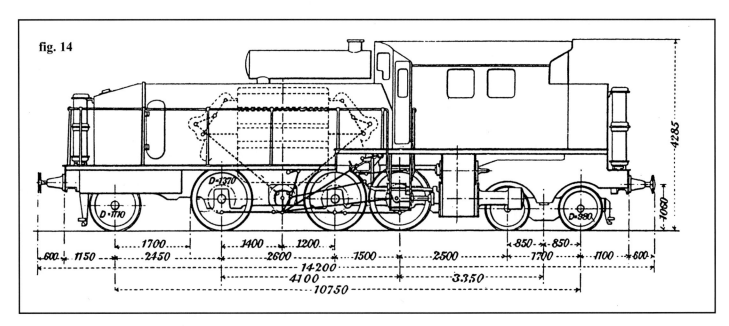

fig. 14

were connected to a system of oscillating links, transforming the power into a rotating motion at the jackshaft, (fig. 15). The starting mechanism was again compressed air, introduced into the outside cylinders. As the driving wheels reached approximately 10 rpm, fuel ignition was activated in the diesel's cylinders. From that moment on the outside cylinders worked as air pumps. They refilled the tanks and supplied the diesel engine with fresh, supercharged air. Further on, those cylinders could act as "motorbrakes" when the locomotive was running downhill hauling a heavy load. For steep gradients, the same cylinders could also work as a booster, assisting the diesel.

Compared to previous similar projects, this locomotive was more successful and test runs on Italian metals proved its reliability. The prototype engine was incorporated as no. D1301.1001 into the FS lists. Together with the Ansaldo Works, the FS management elaborated a large programme for several locomotive types using the Ansaldo princi-

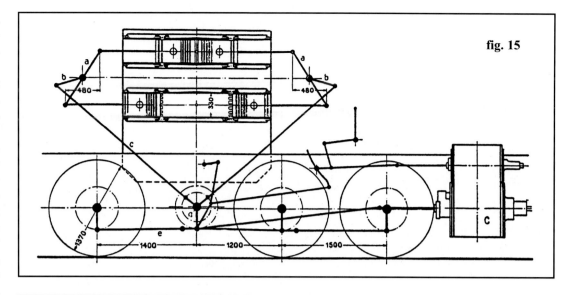

fig. 15

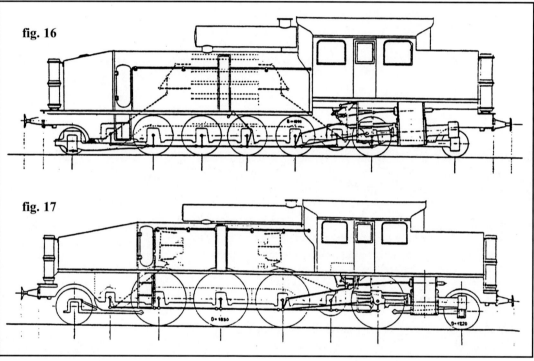

fig. 16

fig. 17

ple, figures 16 and 17. The development of electrification in Italy, however, stopped their translation from the drawing board into practice.

At that period, in Britain the Kitson-Still diesel-steam locomotive was built and successfully tested on the London & North Eastern Railway but it is not my intention not to mention this locomotive further here as its engine didn't work directly on the driving wheels. An intermediate gear wheel was connected between the motor crank axle and the jackshaft, excluding this locomotive from the direct driven "family".

The November 1935 issue of the 'Railway Gazette' presented a project for a three-cylinder 4-6-2 reversible diesel driven passenger locomotive (fig. 18). With a critical eye upon problems with the geared power transmission on the contemporary experimental Ljungström

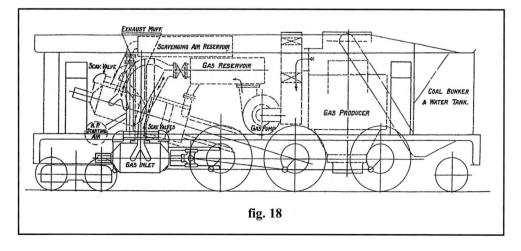

fig. 18

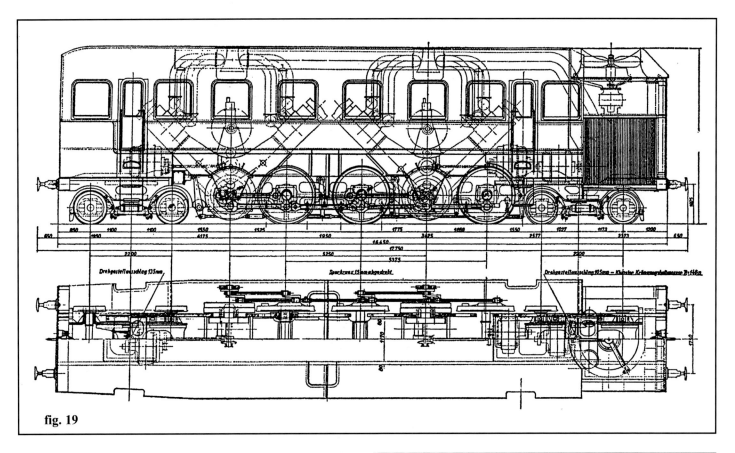

fig. 19

steam turbine locomotive in Great Britain, the anonymous author considered that a suitable gear for high power outputs could not be created and so recommends direct drive as the best alternative. His project features a gas generator for starting, instead of fuel and compressed air.

The Ansaldo locomotive proved to be very useful indeed, however, it was not suitable for long term operation. Neither the complicated and maintenance-heavy articulations nor the compressed air aggregates were likely to contribute to a long lived locomotive able to cope with unexpected situations during hard daily operation. That's perhaps the real reason why O. Günther, Mechanical Engineer at the Maschinenfabrik Esslingen Works returned in 1927 to the initial Klose-Borsig idea, avoiding a supplementary starting circuit such as compressed air or steam.

Fig. 19 shows a large 4-6-4, 2900hp standard gauge passenger locomotive incorporating a pair of reversible two-stroke 4-cylinder Vee engines. At first glance this project appears like a duplicated Borsig-Klose locomotive from 1912. The similarity is doubtless but the main difference to the earlier experiment was the friction couplings incorporated onto the jackshafts (fig. 20) enabling non-load operation of the motors. Power was transmitted from the jackshafts to the driving wheels by coupling rods.

It was 1929 when the Maschinenfabrik Esslingen Works delivered to the Deutsche Reichsbahn a 4-6-4 diesel locomotive with compressed air drive (see Locomotives International magazine issues 12 and 26). Obviously with a very optimistic attitude towards this experiment, but also impressed by the new standardised 4-6-2 express steam locomotives, Esslingen proposed a 4-6-2 express design with 2000mm driving wheels, amalgamating both a direct-drive diesel motor and a compressed air drive, an auxiliary diesel engine being used to run the compressor (fig 21).

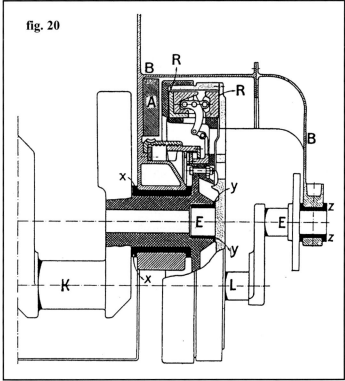

fig. 20

At last, in 1926, electric starting devices were proposed for direct drive locomotives on a Russian project for a large 4-8-4 passenger locomotive, (fig. 22). The main source of power were two horizontal 2-cylinder engines with four opposed, double acting pistons, connected to oscillating links, crank axles and coupling rods, (fig. 23). An auxiliary diesel drove a DC-generator to power an electric motor which acted on a four step geared

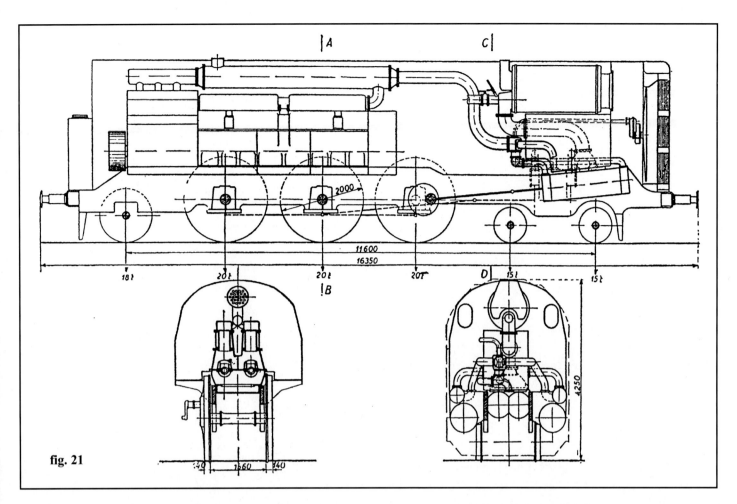

fig. 21

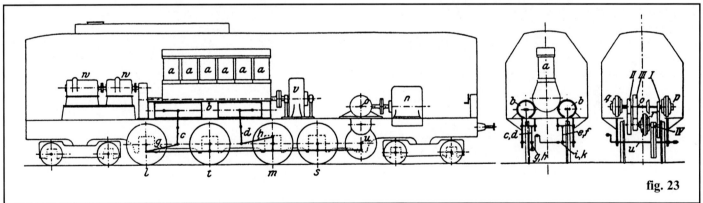

fig. 23

transmission including a jack-shaft at the output. The auxiliary diesel-electric drive would have been used both as a starter and a booster. Amazingly, an additional six wheeled tender was intended to carry the obviously quite large the cooling plant, (fig. 24). An imposing project indeed, but surely also very complicated, which is why it never ran.

Russian railwaymen were certainly true to the direct drive. As an incentive for a possible Russian order directed towards the German locomotive industry, two large locomotives for freight and passenger operation, respectively a 4-8-2 and a 4-10-0 were described in the German publication 'Zeitschrift des Vereins deutscher Ingenieure' in 1930 (figs. 25 & 26). E. Schwetter, Mechanical Engineer at the Technical University of Berlin firmly considered the direct drive as superior to electric, hydraulic or mechanical drives. The difference to all the previous projects

being in this case mainly the small vertical steam boiler also mounted on the locomotive frames. The power unit consisted of two supercharged double-acting two-cylinder motors working on the two central pairs of driving wheels. Compressed air was the starter, kept in a large reservoir placed over the motors. To facilitate ignition, especially at low environmental temperatures, the motors would have been pre-heated from a steam boiler. The air inlet to the cylinders was pre-heated in a heat exchanger too, at the boiler's exhaust. The motor's water cooling system could alternatively be switched to the boiler or to the cooling circuit and as soon as the diesels worked the cooling/heating water circuit was switched to the cooling fan placed at one of the locomotive's extremities.

The last time a pure direct drive locomotive was put into practice, in 1933 in Germany, Humboldt-Deutz Works were the

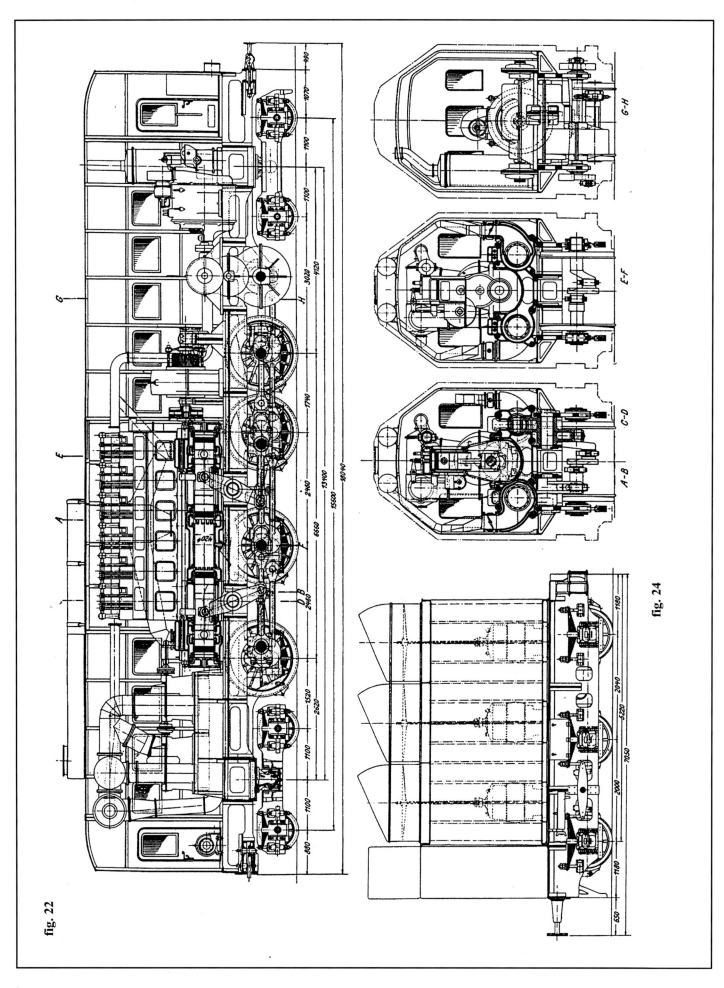

fig. 22

fig. 24

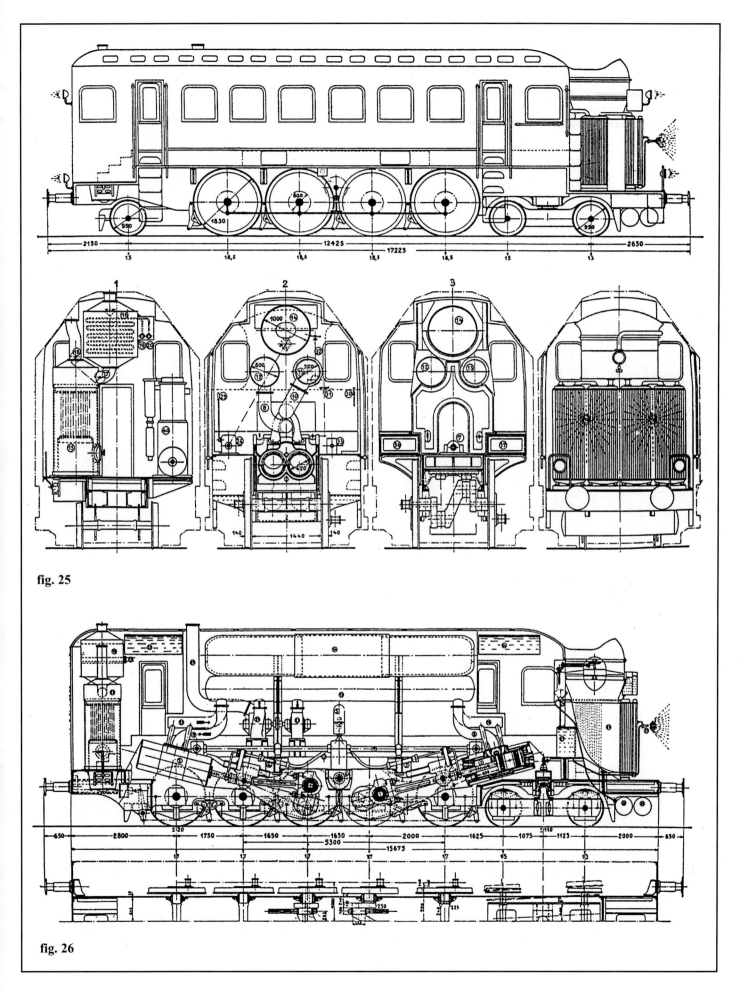

fig. 25

fig. 26

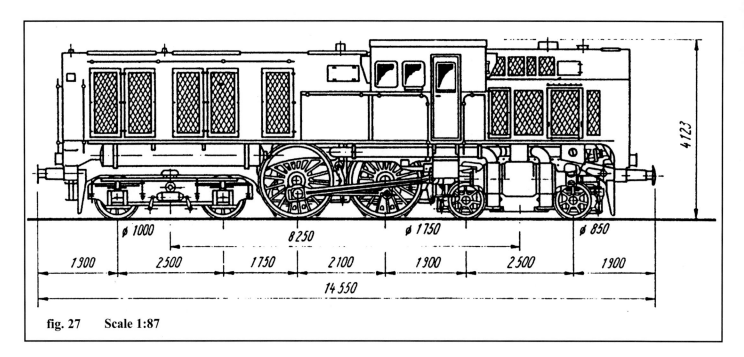

fig. 27   Scale 1:87

constructors, (fig. 27). The original Borsig-Klose philosophy from 1912 was generally re-introduced in this project, but essentially improved. It was a three cylinder 4-4-4 passenger locomotive with a two stroke, double acting diesel engine, the cylinders having the same horizontal placement as for a steam locomotive at one extremity. Starting was allowed again by an auxiliary compressed air system, from tanks supplied by a supplementary diesel-compressor unit. It became the only successful direct drive diesel locomotive, running satisfactorily for several years on German tracks performing the same duties as steam locomotives.

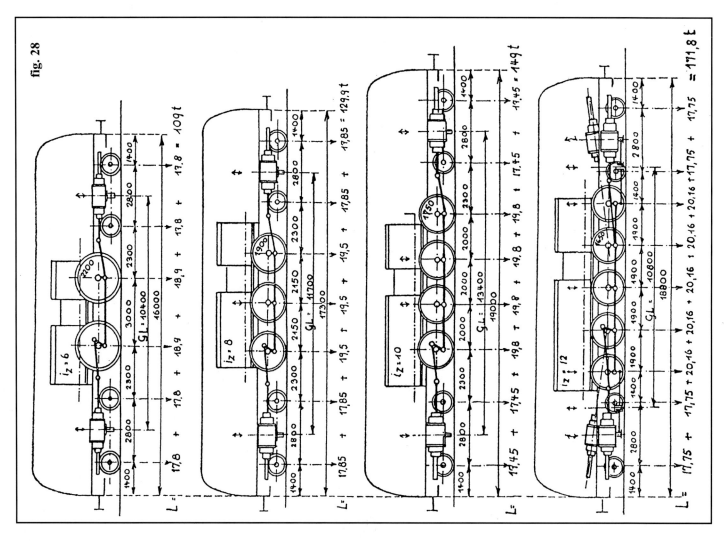

fig. 28

However, the Reichsbahn administration couldn't decide whether to purchase this unique prototype, the locomotive remaining in the ownership of the Humboldt Deutz Works until it was destroyed during the WW2.

Its reliability encouraged some constructors, such as Dr. Max Mayer from the Maschinenfabrik Esslingen Works, to elaborate a standardisation diagram for several types of direct driven locomotives as late as 1942/43, (fig. 28). Unfortunately, political and economic circumstances were not very favourable to such ideas at that time...

The Russian engineers also continued studies upon direct drive, in spite of some remarkable experiences with diesel mechanical and diesel electric locomotives on their lines from the mid 1920s. In 1935 L. M. Maisel, a student of the Electro-Mechanical Institute in Moscow proposed an original diesel-steam drive: his principle followed the classic steam locomotive, but with a major difference made in the design of the cylinders. They would have been used simultaneously for both diesel and steam operation with double acting, opposed pistons. Starting would be as a normal steam locomotive until an "ignition speed" of 15km/h was reached, when the steam supply to the central combustion chamber between the opposing piston heads would be stopped and replaced by diesel fuel. In this way the motor continued to work as a steam engine on one side of the pistons, the other side working as an internal combustion engine. The system was closely related to the British Still locomotive but Maisel's locomotive would work continuously as a hybrid engine while the Britons used steam power for starting only. Maisel also hoped to record significant coal savings at higher speed ranges due to the contribution of the diesel motor.

Maisel graduated as a Mechanical Engineer, his proposals were accepted and a prototype was built. A conventional locomotive boiler interchangeable with those used on the 2-6-2 class S passenger locos supplied steam to a pair of 460mm cylinders supported outside the driving wheels by a special device at the centre of the running gear. Motion from the pistons was transmitted to jack-shafts at either end of the 2-8-2 set of driving wheels, the wheels being connected to these jack-shafts by coupling rods. The internal combustion engine was supplied with supercharged air from a steam turbine blower placed in front of the boiler, over the buffer beam.

In 1939 Maisel's steam-diesel locomotive, intended for express duties at a power output of 3000hp, was outshopped by the Voroshilovgrad Works in Lugansk, (fig. 29). The decision was made for such a size of a locomotive, as it was intended to compare it with the large 2-8-4 express class JS (Joseph Stalin) locomotives then in use.

In the beginning, test runs were quite satisfactory, except for leaking in the steam system of the power plant, an anomaly for which a remedy never could be found. During 1946 cracks appeared inside the cylinders and further on synchronicity failures of both power circuits reduced the expected hopes of fuel economy. The locomotive was retired in 1948 and interestingly, it was preserved.

Two other locomotives following the same principle, both of 2-10-2 wheel arrangement, were built in Russia at that time. The first one came out of the Kolomna Works in 1939 and the other one again from Lugansk, in 1948. The novelty of these locomotives was the replacement of oil fuel by gas for diesel operation,

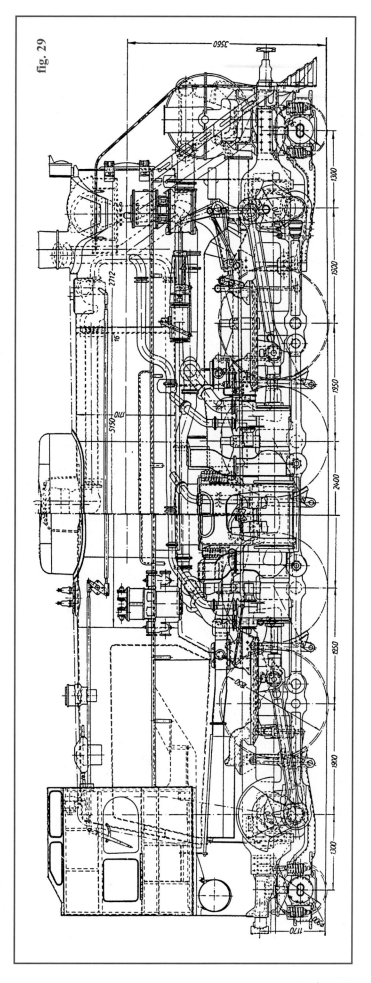

fig. 29

the gas producer being mounted on a 12-wheel condensing tender, (fig. 30). This experiment was later re-introduced onto Soviet railways during the 1950s, when some diesel-electric loco multiple units were experimentally attached to a supplementary gas generator tender.

Compared to the 2-8-2 the two 2-10-2s were less successful, both of them generating a high level of vibration when running at low speed. Furthermore, ignition failures could never be managed and the experiments were cancelled, the locomotives soon being scrapped. The Russian locomotives working on the Maisel principle were in fact hybrid constructions, semi-diesels with direct power transmission to the driving wheels.

We have followed the development of a special aspect of locomotives with internal combustion, a quite long trip over many years and countries. We could also say, a development followed by several failures, but not at all unsuccessful as it nevertheless made an important contribution to the maturing of the diesel engine. For the directly driven locomotive itself, however, this principle had little chance for the future. Of course, it offered the advantage of avoiding an intermediate transmission between the power unit and driving wheels. Maintenance costs could possibly have been reduced in this way, but on the other hand, the problem of starting a diesel engine under load, never could be satisfactory solved. Neither friction couplings nor other systems could avoid another evil, that of very high levels of vibration. The explosive ignition inside the cylinders always remained a source of vibration and the absence of an intermediate drive meant that it could never be absorbed. It is said that working on the footplate of the Borsig-Klose engine from 1912 was a the driver's nightmare!

Today, the direct drive for diesel locomotives is history but the many unfulfilled projects are an exciting reason to follow the great and fascinating story of locomotives that were never built.

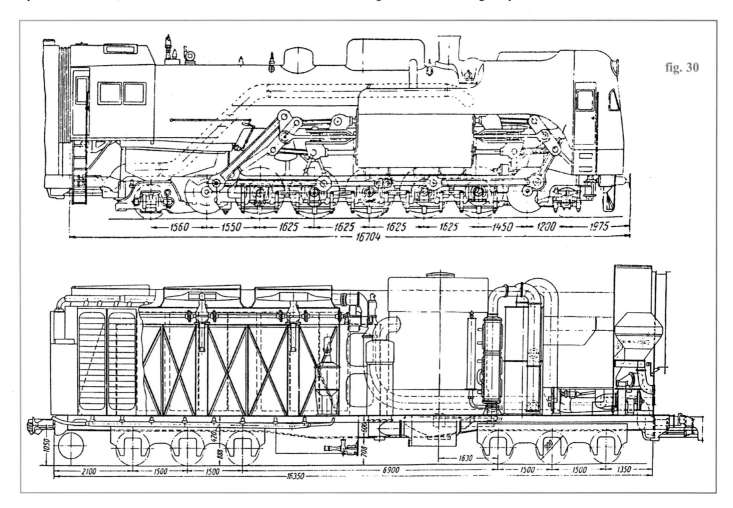

fig. 30

Sources:

The British Internal Combustion Locomotive 1894-1940, Brian Webb, David & Charles 1973

Lokomotivbau und Dampftechnik, Wolfgang Stoffels, Birkhäuser Verlag, Basel, Stuttgart, 1976

Organ für die Fortschritte des Eisenbahnwesens, 1912

Revue Générale des Chemins de Fer. Application du moteur a hydrocarbures à la traction sur voies ferrées, M. Brillié, Paris, 1924

Von Lok zu Lok, Wolfgang Messerschmidt, Franckh'sche Verlagsbuchhandlung, Stuttgart, 1969

Diesel Lokomotiven, G.V. Lomonossoff, VDI-Verlag, Berlin, 1929

The Railway Gazette, Internal Combustion Locomotives, London, 1923

Zeitschrift des Bereins deutscher Ingenieure, Berlin, 1927 & 1930

Glasers Annalen, 1930 (Reprint), Georg Siemens Verlagsbuchhandlung, Berlin

Diesellokomotiven deutscher Eisenbahnen, Wolfgang Glatte, Alba/Transpress Verlag, 1981

Diesellok Raritäten, Wolfgang Messerschmidt, Franckh'sche Verlagsbuchhandlung, Stuttgart, 1980

Dutch Narrow Gauge Diesels *by Paul Engelbert*

In the 1930s MBS DII with trailer AB 12 awaits departure in front of the standard gauge railway station at Nijmegen.
Author's collection.

In the first half of the 20th century Holland was covered with narrow gauge lines. The lines varied from classic steam tramways to real narrow gauge local railway systems. An example of the latter category is the MBS (Maashuurtspoorweg or Maas Local Railway), which opened its 64 km long, 1067 mm gauge line between Venlo and Nijmegen on January 1st 1913.

The line was originally steam-operated but the financial crisis forced the MBS to search for more economical traction forms. As there was no money to buy new diesel railcars the MBS had to improvise and it was decided to transform one of the luggage vans into a diesel-electric locomotive. So in 1932 four-axle wooden luggage van number EL106 was fitted with a 75hp diesel engine and a dynamo, which provided the power for both 38hp electric motors in one of the bogies. The locomotive only had one cab. On the other end it was short-coupled with passenger coach number AB14. This coach was slightly rebuilt and fitted with a small cab on the rear end, from where the diesel locomotive could be operated. The combination of locomotive D I and trailer AB14 formed a unit which always stayed together. Sometimes an additional passenger or freight wagon was coupled behind the trailer or the locomotive. In the latter case the locomotive found itself in the middle of the train.

In 1935 a similar unit (locomotive D II and trailer AB12) came into service and in 1936 a third one (D III and AB13) followed. Locomotive D III was fitted with a more powerful diesel engine (120hp) and had two cabs, so it could also run without its trailer.

Finally in 1937 and 1939 the MBS rebuilt luggage coaches EL103 and EL102 into diesel engines D IV and D V. These were real locomotives with cabs on both ends and not short-coupled with a passenger coach. They both had a 240hp diesel engine and in both bogies two electric motors (so four motors in total). These powerful engines were in the first place built for hauling heavy freight trains, however, they could sometimes also be seen with heavy passenger trains of up to 12 bogie passenger coaches.

MBS diesel engines D I - D V were the first and only really successful narrow gauge diesel locomotives in the Netherlands. They were in service without any problems. Only in 1926 for unknown reasons were the trailers AB13 and AB14 swapped over.

During the liberation of this part of the Netherlands in the Autumn of 1944 the MBS was heavily damaged. After the Second World War the railway was not brought back into service again and buses took over the passenger and freight traffic. The line was dismantled and a large part of the damaged rolling stock, amongst which were the five diesel locomotives, was sold to the Rotterdamsche Tramweg Maatschappi (RTM).

The RTM operated an extensive narrow gauge minor railway network on the islands south-west of Rotterdam. In Rotterdam the MBS diesel engines D I - D V were gradually repaired and taken into service again.

Only two of them (D I and D II) remained short-coupled with a trailer. The trailer of D III (AB 12) was destroyed during the war and the loco itself was apparently also heavily damaged. The RTM restored D III, gave it a new 286hp diesel engine and took it into service as a normal locomotive with the number M68[II]. It was the most powerful locomotive of the RTM.

The RTM did not have much luck with the former MBS locomotives as three of them were destroyed by fire and another one collided with a standard gauge steam engine of the state railways. In 1949 the RTM rebuilt the burned-out M68 (the first one) into an almost completely new diesel locomotive, which however looked exactly like the original wooden MBS-loco. It was fitted with a 150hp diesel engine and renumbered M67. Instead of the original eight it now only had four driven wheels.

Also the burned-out M69 was rebuilt but this time into a very modern looking locomotive, which by no means looked like the old wooden MBS-diesels. Instead of brown teak wood it was

M65 with trailer AB422 in the station of Middelharnis Dorp around 1960. By this time this combination was the only motive power on the island of Goeree. It was used for the remaining freight traffic on the short line from the town of Middelharnis to the nearby harbour.

Author's collection.

made completely of steel and painted bright red and white with aluminium stripes. Also it was fitted with a completely new 200hp diesel engine and a new generator. The new engine was numbered M1805 and taken into service in 1952.

The next year the crashed D68ᴵᴵ was rebuilt the same way but kept its diesel engine, which was still as good as new. It was renumbered M1806. Finally in 1957 a third similar locomotive (M1807) was constructed. This was a complete new one, which the RTM built from scrap, using the bogies of a former MBS passenger coach.

The RTM now had three modernised diesel engines and it was planned to rebuild the last old fashioned one, diesel engine M67, the same way. Around 1960 the reconstruction started twice but each time the work was immediately abandoned due to an acute lack of motive power. Eventually M67 kept its original wooden appearance until the very end.

Since the 1950s the RTM have given their modern red and white buses, railcars and locomotives names of wildlife species in the region. M1805 was called 'Meeuw' (Seagull), M1806 'Bergeend' (Duck) and M1807 'Scholekster' (Oyster-catcher). Together with the name, a large drawing of these birds was painted on both sides of the locomotives. The old fashioned wooden M67 did not get the honour of being officially renamed after a bird species, however, because of its brown colour the locomotive was sometimes called 'Mus' (Sparrow).

The four 'real' diesel locomotives M67 and M1805 - 1807 mainly ran with passenger trains on the lines from Rotterdam to Oostvoorne and Hellevoetsluis. They remained in service until the last days of the RTM railway services in 1966.

Afterwards M1805 was bought by a museum organisation and transferred to the RTM museum railway, which is now operating a 5 km long line near Ouddorp, on the island of Goeree. The locomotive was recently restored and is now in service on the museum railway. The wooden M67, which was the last reminder of the original MBS locomotives, went to the national railway museum in Utrecht in 1967. A few years ago it was transferred to the RTM museum railway, where it is at present being restored to working order. Soon it will be possible for representatives of both the original and the modernised version of the narrow gauge diesel locomotives to be admired in front of passenger or freight trains on the museum railway along the Dutch coast.

Renumbering and rebuilding scheme MBS-RTM							
MBS			**RTM**			**In RTM Service**	**Remarks**
Loco	Trailer	Type	Loco	Trailer	Type		
DI	AB14	Bo'2'+2'2'	M65	AB422	Bo'2'+2'2'	1947-1962	destroyed by fire
DII	AB12	Bo'2'+2'2'	M66	AB423	Bo'2'+2'2'	1947-1961	scrapped 1967
DIII	AB13	Bo'2'+2'2'	M68ᴵᴵ	-	Bo'Bo	1949-1963	collision M1806
DIV	-	Bo'Bo'	M68	-	Bo'Bo'	1946-1947	destroyed by fire M67
DV	-	Bo'Bo'	M69	-	Bo'Bo'	1948-1951	destroyed by fire M1805

New RTM diesel locomotives				
Numbers	Rebuilt From	Type	In Service	Remarks
M67	M68	Bo'2'	1949-1966	via national railway museum to RTM museum railway
M1805	M69	Bo'Bo'	1952-1966	to RTM museum railway
M1806	M68ᴵᴵ	Bo'Bo'	1953-1966	scrapped 1967
M1807	-	Bo'Bo'	1956-1964	scrapped 1967

M67 shunting in the Rosestraat in Rotterdam, where the narrow gauge trains of the RTM had their terminus.
Author's collection.

M1805 with a passenger train for Rotterdam in the station of Oostvoorne. The last two passenger coaches were also bought from the MBS. On the left are two red and white passenger coaches from the narrow gauge Arnhem - Zeist line, on the right a special freight wagon for express goods.
Author's collection.

M1805 was looking as good as new when Paul Engelbert photographed her on the RTM museum railway near Ouddorp on April 16th 2001.

The Dieselization of the Central Railway of Peru *by Ian Thomson*

1. Introduction and Summary

Perú's Central Railway was dieselized in the early 1960's, after the management and directors of the Peruvian Corporation had convinced themselves of the technical feasibility of diesel operation at high altitudes by the successful introduction of main line diesels on the Southern Railway, which, like the Central Railway, was run by the Peruvian. Once the diesels arrived, most of the steam locomotives they replaced were rapidly dispensed with. However, dieselization could not save the Peruvian from effective bankruptcy and the company was taken over by the State in 1972. The financial woes of the Peruvian meant that it was not in a position to buy additional diesels and the State takeover coincided with a brief resurgence of steam activity in the Lima-El Callao zone. This came to an end once further diesels arrived, ordered by the State owned Empresa Nacional de Ferrocarriles del Perú (ENAFER). Dieselization brought lower costs and a certain speeding up of operations, but capacity increases were limited as long as the dead end tracks of the zig-zags remained unlengthened.

On 28th September 1997, Villares Co-Co no. 705 negotiates the first zig-zag above San Bartolomé, in typical mountain zone scenery.

2. High altitudes and low profitability delay dieselization

Until 1963, the Central Railway of Perú (FCC) was virtually completely steam worked, as regards main line freight and passenger operations. The only diesel powered locomotives on the FCC's books were six diesel shunters, most of which had recently been transferred from the Paita-Piura Railway which, like the FCC, was owned by the then Canadian registered Peruvian Transport Corporation. There were also six Sentinel railcars converted from steam and four built as diesel powered units by Wickhams. There were also four survivors of a small fleet of electric locomotives, taken over with the Lima Railway, and used in yard operations in the Lima-El Callao zone.

The Peruvian Corporation, still essentially a British managed

Locomotives of three generations are housed in the motive power depot at Chosica on 15th August 1999. On the left is 1974 vintage M.L.W. built 950hp Bo-Bo No. 415; in the middle is preserved Andes type 2-8-0 No. 206; and at the right is the omnipresent Villares built 1986 vintage Co-Co No. 705.

enterprise even though the company´s headquarters had been switched to Canada, ran the two major railways operating in Perú, i.e. the FCC and the Southern Railway (FCS). For the FCS, a fleet of six ALCO/GE DL-500-C (World) class Co-Cos had been delivered in 1956. They were working reliably with operating costs less than half those of equally powered steam locomotives. Then in 1958, also from ALCO/GE a single DL-531 model Co-Co was delivered to the FCS. The latter was numbered 300 and the former 500 to 505.

Quite obviously, the Peruvian (as it was known in Perú) was concerned about the effect of high altitudes on diesel operations. The highest point on the FCS´s main line is at 4 477 meters above sea level, whilst the FCC reaches 4 781 meters. Fawcett notes that the Worlds were derated from 1 800 hp to 1 300 hp for high altitude operation. FCS sources indicate the DL-531 was derated from 900 hp to 675 hp. It is interesting to observe that the U.S. owned and managed Cerro de Pasco Railway Co. was ordering steam locomotives as late as 1957, due to having the same doubts as the Peruvian about diesels at high altitudes. The Peruvian itself was seriously considering buying more Beyer Garratts in 1955.

A derated World had aproximately the same horsepower rating as an Andes 2-8-0, and could do what an Andes could do at very much lower operating costs. Once this was was proven to be the case, the writing was on the wall for steam, both on the FCS and the FCC. The Peruvian was by no means a wealthy company.

On a wintery 28th September 1997, ALCO Co-Co No. 607, one of the pioneer 1963 built batch, rides on the turntable at Casapalca.

The FCC´s operating ratio for 1952/53 (which seems to have been an exceptionally bad year) was as high as 111%. The ratio for the entire Corporation, which took in several unimportant short lines which, at the very best, could only have been marginally profitable, must have been even worse. See table 1. Thus even though it was in a bad condition to finance investment in new locomotives, it had to do all it could to get the ratio below 100%. Complete information is not available as to how well it succeded, but it seems to have made out quite well but not well enough. With a ratio of 102% in 1964 the FCC still had a negative rate of return, even though the returns from the diesels themselves might

A reminder of the era when, each day, a passenger train ran from Lima to Huancayo, and another in the opposite direction. Here we see them crossing each other, at Casapalca. On the left hand side of the picture, the train in charge of M.L.W. built No. 617 is, I remember, bound for Lima and is backing down the zig-zag. The photo was taken in March 1988, when the Sendero Luminoso guerillas were threatening to take over the country.

DL-535Bs, which incidentally were equipped with British manufactured (AEI) traction motors and generators. Steam locomotive operations promptly plummeted, from over 90% of all train kilometers in 1963 to less than half in 1964. See table 2.

The first steam locomotives to be withdrawn were the relatively few remaining elderly and non-standard ones and at mid 1964, all the 31 Andes 2-8-0s and the two closely related type 100 2-8-0s were still on the books. See table 3. However, many were laid up at the Chosica motive power depot and at the Guadalupe shops in El Callao. By August 1964, Andes locomotives had started to be despatched to the Fundición Callao for scrapping, even before the last remaining ALCO 2-8-2 (53) and Rogers 2-8-0 (70) were similarly dealt with. Twelve Andes locomotives were delivered to the Fundición between 24th August and 28th October. 219 seems to have been the first to go.

It is obvious that the Peruvian had no doubt that its newly acquired diesels were up to the jobs assigned to them. Were it not to have been so convinced, it surely would have kept its Andes 2-8-0s hanging around in store a little longer, in spite of the Corporation being in need of all the money it could raise by selling scrap.

Some more money was raised by renting out some surplus Andes 2-8-0s to the Cerro de Pasco concern. Locomotives 206, 210, 215, 226, 227 and 228 were so hired out at the end of June 1964. (A few years later, the successors to the Peruvian would be hiring in 2-8-0s from Cerro de Pasco.)

By 1967, only five Andes 2-8-0s were left in stock and of these 210 and 227 were withdrawn on 18th April, leaving just 203, 206 and 216. By mid 1968, only 206 remained in active service. It would appear that the current 206 is really 203, which is the number stamped on a part of the valve gear and consistent with a hand written remark in a FCC traction department stock list (although not consistent with all such remarks). A newspaper

On 15th August 1999, the Sunday tourist train is marshalled at San Bartolomé by Montreal built Bo-Bo No. 415. It was later to leave triple headed, behind the super power combination of locomotives Nos. 415, 702 and 706, for the downhill trip to Lima.

have been satisfactory. Thus dieselization did not prevent the company being auctioned in 1972. It might even have heralded that sad event, by increasing the amount of money which had to be repaid to the creditors.

3. The decision to dieselize, and its effects on operations and on the steam fleet

In 1962, the Peruvian invited tenders for diesel locomotives to work over the FCC and ALCO was selected as the preferred supplier. Orders were signed for three 1 200 hp DL-535B model Co-Cos and twelve 2 400 hp DL-560D Co-Cos. These horsepower ratings are at sea level; at 4 760 meters above sea level, the DL-535Bs developed 900 hp and the DL-560Ds 1 835 hp. They entered service as from the end of October 1963, starting with the

Table 1: Basic characteristics of railways operated by the Peruvian Corporation, circa 1964					
Railway	Route km	Traffic in thousands of metric tons	Average haul in km	Net ton/kms in thousands	Operating Ratio
Central	346	1 316 300	156	205 343	102
Matarani-La Joya*	62	263 400	62	16 331	124
Pacasmayo	131	1 350	95	128	129
Paita	62	25 400	14	348	116
Southern	862	574 300	248	142 426	110
Trujillo	95	203 000	15	2 944	112

* Operated by the Peruvian Corporation on behalf of the Peruvian government.

Source: Jane's World Railways, 1965-66

Table 2: Central Railway: train kms. by motive power in the early 1960s			
Type of traction	1962	1963	1964
Steam	90.23%	91.84%	47.88%
Diesel	7.93%	6.52%	50.14%
Electric	1.84%	1.64%	1.98%

Source: Jane's World Railways, 1965-66

report claimed that an ex-Peruvian employee had 206 hidden out of sight for safe keeping until the Peruvian was nationalized. However this is clearly not the case.

DL-560D 602 was written off on 2 December 1965, presumably following accident damage. It is deduced (although not proven) that 600 was then renumbered 602, so that the series could start at "1" rather than at "0".

The fleet of higher powered locomotives was inadequate to completely dieselize main line operations. Hence, three more DL-560Ds were ordered and outshopped by ALCO in April 1965. These were the last genuine ALCO products received by the FCC, and were assigned numbers 612 to 614 (makers nos. 84752 to 84754).

4. Steam's final fling and new diesel orders by ENAFER

The Peruvian Corporation was fast becoming one of the last privately owned railway companies operating in Latin America. Highway competition was one reason for their downfall, but it was not the only one. Governments undermined their financial situation by making it difficult to lay off workers, by controlling freight rates, and so on. By 1972, the Peruvian was ready to throw in the towel, even though, since renegotiating its agreement with the government in 1928, it held perpetual rights over Railway. However the property of the bankrupt company was auctioned on 30th November 1972. Not surprisingly, the only bid was made by the newly formed State-owned Empresa Nacional de Ferrocarriles del Perú (ENAFER).

It would appear that the traffic on hand at the beginning of the early 1970s was too much for the existing diesel fleet to handle. However, the bankrupt Peruvian Corporation was in no condition to buy any more diesels. 206 was pressed back into service on freight turns between El Callao and Chosica. The sole surviving Bagnall 0-6-0ST, 30 was returned to shunt the yards in El Callao and two (I think) Hunslet saddle tanks brought in from the FCS. The minute Beyer, Peacock 0-4-0WT 20 might have been fired up too. All other FCC steam locomotives had been sold for scrap, apart from one 0-4-0WT transferred to the Pacasmayo railway and another donated to a Childrens' park in Lima. sold for scrap, apart from one 0-4-0WT transferred to the Pacasmayo railway and another donated to a Childrens' park in Lima.

A mechanical engineer was sent to La Oroya and Cerro de Pasco to inspect available Cerro de Pasco Andes type 2-8-0s (some of which were still in use) and Cerro's locomotives numbered 71, 76 and 77 rented in, mainly to work in the yards around El Callao. However, in 1973, David Wardale recalls that the Huancayo-Lima passenger train on which he was travelling

The Central Railway has not always carried just freight comprising inputs and products of the mining sector. Villares built Co-Co No. 705 is heading uphill to La Oroya, hauling cars and crates in the first wagon, whilst ALCO built No. 610 is going down with copper, placed over the bogies rather than in the middle of the wagon, where its weight might buckle the frame. The date is 23rd May 1992.

had its diesel unhooked at La Oroya and replaced by a Cerro 2-8-0 for the rest of the run. He surmises that it had returned to La Oroya for maintenance and was working its way back south. ENAFER engineers remember that maintenance was carried out at the Guadalupe shops, so maybe David's lucky strike had some other explanation.

This brief return to steam did not last long, since as soon ENAFER took over, it set about ordering more diesels. These were mainly similar to the existing ALCOs, but built by the Montreal Locomotive Works, since ALCO had by then ceased to trade. See table 4.

The only other diesel locomotives bought new for the FCC by ENAFER were some General Motors model JT-26CW-2B 3 000 hp Co-Cos built by Villares in Brazil. Their high altitude rating was 2 400 hp. Five were built in 1986 and given running numbers as 701 to 705. However, 703 was put out of service by terrorist action a few years later. (Its remains lie in a shed in the Guadalupe workshop area.) It was replaced by a similar machine, Villares 4203, ENAFER's 706. These are the only FCC locomotives with a cabin at each end, which constitutes a dubious advantage. Although obviating the need for turntables, visibility from the driving cabin being used is somewhat inferior to the ALCO's when pushing up zig-zags, and the extra cabin takes up space, which is at a premium on the dead end necks of the zig-zags.

The Villares locomotives were the only General Motors products acquired new for the FCC but the taking over of most of the ex Cerro de Pasco railway operations in 1997 brought into the fold most of Cerro's G.M. GR12 Co-Cos. These, numbered 31 to 39 by Cerro de Pasco (and later, after nationalization, by Centromin) are currently being renumbered by Ferrovías Centro

A manoeuvre that would probably not be approved of by the A.A.R. rule book takes places on one of the zig-zags in May 1992. The train has to be split, since it is too long to be accommodated in the dead end. The photo was taken from the roof of the Villares Co-Co that was providing the power.

Andino, which took over the FCC in November 1999, by the addition of 500.

ENAFER had previously renumbered certain FCC diesel locomotives. DL-535Bs numbered 530, 531 and 532 became 433, 431 and 432, respectively. Also, yard shunters numbered 500 and 507 became 401 and 402. Andes 2-8-0 206 was even assigned the number 940, but never carried it. In the latter 1980s, 206 was transferred to Huancayo, either (according to with whom one speaks) for intermittent local freight working to Jauja, or for safe keeping away from the sometimes salty and moist air of the El Callao area. It was seemingly used at Huancayo, and also inexpertly looked after, judging by the lime which covered large sections of its boiler cladding. In 1988 the locomotive department at Huancayo confirmed to the FCC´s head office that it was being kept there, whereby the head office automatically presumed it must be a 3 foot gauge locomotive. So in the stock returns for that year it appears in the 3 foot gauge section.

5. Efficiency gains from dieselization

What were the returns from dieselization? We have already mentioned that it didn´t save the Peruvian Corporation from going under the auctioneer's hammer. Unit operating costs for diesel locomotives were significantly less than those of the steam locomotives they replaced, but on the other hand the diesels were more expensive to buy than similarly powered steam ones, at least in the 1950s. Diesel operation did not make possible very much greater train loadings than with steam, except over the relatively flat and non-critical Lima-Chosica section, where the ruling grade is only 2.79%. The ruling grade over the mountain section is 4.37%, and there the Beyer Garratts could haul 340 tons going upwards (or northwards in local ralwaymen's terms). This equated to 12 wagons, presumably not all fully laden. No more could be taken because of the length of the dead end necks of the zig-zags. So even if the diesels had greater low speed tractive power, they could still not handle trains of greater length, except insomuch that an ALCO diesel was shorter than an FCC Garratt

and would have been able to release space for an extra wagon. However, they would have speeded up operations and, hence, have contributed thereby to increasing line capacity. In the 1980s, works were carried out to lengthen these necks.

In 1997, ENAFER budgetted for 233.7 million ton-km of Centromin freight, 34.3 ton-km million for other freight and 3.4 million passenger-km. Revising these figures to exclude traffic over the ex-Cerro de Pasco section (which they are assumed to include), the raw total number of traffic units would have been approximately 192 million. This was to be handled with a fleet of 15 main line locomotives (not counting those transferred from Centromin). See table 4. In 1955, 164 million ton-km of freight and 122 million passenger-km were handled.

Since most of the freight goes downward, whilst the passenger traffic is evenly balanced, it would give a distorted picture to simply add ton-km and passenger-km to get a number of total traffic units. Multiplying the number of freight ton-km, for each year, by 1.5 to allow for the inherent need to haul uphill returning empty wagons, one calculates that in 1955, the total volume amounted to 368 million revised traffic units, as against 286 million for 1997.

Hence in 1997, each main line locomotive handled 19 million revised traffic units, as opposed to 10 million in 1955. There defintely was been an improvement in the physical productivity of each locomotive, but over a 42 year span, the rate of improvement was only 1.6% per year.

6. Diesel shunting locomotives

Finally, some brief words on yard locomotives. In 1948 the FCC took delivery of a single G.E. 44 ton 300 hp B-B switcher, but, even though it appears to have been relatively successful, never bought another. It was numbered 500. The next to arrive was 510, a Hunslet 500 hp diesel mechanical 0-6-0 built in 1952 and placed in service in 1953.

Then at the end of the 1950s, more shunters arrived from Paita railway, which was being wound down. Two of these were 0-8-0

Table 4: Numbering and basic characteristics of Central Railway diesel electric locomotives

Number series	Previous number series	Builder and builder's model number	Year entered service	Wheel arrangement	Drawbar Horsepower at sea level	Maximum axle load (kgs)
401	500	G.E. (44 ton switcher)	1948	B-B	270	10 400
411-415	n/a	M.L.W., DL-532B	1974	Bo-Bo	950	17 350
413-433	*530-532	ALCO, DL-535B	1963	Co-Co	900	13 516
434-436	n/a	M.L.W., DL-535B	1974	Co-Co	900	13 516
601-614	n/a	ALCO, DL-560D	1963 and 1965	Co-Co	2 400	18 323
615-619	n/a	M.L.W., DL-560D	1974	Co-Co	2 400	18 583
701-706	n/a	Villares (GM) JT26CW-2B	1986	Co-Co	3 000	20 000

* These locomotives were not renumbered in the same order.

Table 3: Central Railway locomotive stock by type, 1957 - 1999

Type of locomotive	1957	1960	1962	1963	1964	1965	1968	1985	1999
Type 20 (Beyer, Peacock 0-4-0WT)	3	3	2	2	1	1	1	0	0
Type 30 (Bagnall 0-6-0ST)	3	3	3	3	2	1	1	0	0
Type 50 (ALCO 2-8-2)	4	3	3	3a	1	0	0	0	0
Type 60 (North British 2-8-0TT)	2	1	0	0	0	0	0	0	0
Type 70 (Rogers 2-8-0)	4	3	2a	2a	1	0	0	0	0
Type 80 (ALCO S160 type 2-8-0)	2	2	2	2	2	0	0	0	0
Type 100 (Andes with 4'8"wheels)	2	2	2	2	2	0	0	0	0
Type 200 (Andes 2-8-0)	31	31	31	31	31	15b	3	1	0c
Type 400 (2-8-2+2-8-2T Garratt)	2	2	2	2	2	2	0	0	0
Electric yard/local	6	4	4	4	4	0	0	0	0
Diesel shunter series 500	1	1	3	3	3	3	3	2	0
Diesel shunter series 510	1	1	1	1	1	1	1	0	0
Diesel shunter series 520		2	2	2	2	2	2	0	0
Main line diesel series 530				3d	3	3	3	3	1
Main line diesel series 600				1	12	15	14e	14	7
Main line diesel series 411								5	5
Main line diesel series 434								3	2
Main line diesel series 615								5	1
Main line diesel series 701									5f

a Withdrawal already authorized.
b 5 in service, 10 in store.
c No. 206 was not officially included in stock, probably due to the approaching privatization of ENAFER.
d Delivered in October 1963.
e No. 602 already withdrawn, presumably due to accident damage.
f Does not count No. 703.

variants of 510, and received numbers 520 and 521. (The Hunslet works numbers for the three were, respectively, 4002, 4000 and 4001.) Finally, in 1963 two more elderly Hunslet shunters arrived from Paita. 505 was a 165 hp 0-6-0 mechanical dating from 1938 (maker's number 1988). 507 was a more modern version of the same model, uprated to 204 hp, with a Gardner rather than a McLaren engine, and very similar to British Railways' shunters numbered in the 11136 (later D2550) series. 500 and 507 were still in stock in the late 1980s.

Acknowledgements

The author acknowledges the help and encouragement for the elaboration of this article given by Mr. Luis Rosales and Mr. Raúl Rosales (both ex-General Managers of ENAFER), Mr. Armando Melendez, ex-ENAFER employee and currently in charge of the accounting department of the Autoridad Autónomo del Tren Eléctrico, by Mr. Henry Posner III (Chairman of the Rairoad Development Corporation) and by Messrs. Jack Roberson and Manuel Pinto (General Manager and Rolling Stock Maintenance Chief, respectively, of Ferrovías Central Andino)

The McKeen Project

William R McKeen was the right man, in the right place, at the right time - nearly. Had some of these conditions been only slightly different, fleets of motorised railcars might have come earlier than they did. But McKeen, sometime Superintendent of Motive Power to the Union Pacific RR, was a shade too early and his fuse was a mite too short for him to play more than a modest part in the evolution of railway technology.

The historical 'firsts' in railway history are not easy to establish, partly because of the difficulty of reaching at satisfactory and agreed definitions. Internal-combustion propulsion is a particularly fraught area given its wide range of fuels, motor forms, transmission systems and vehicle configurations which range from rail-borne charabancs to Deltics, HSTs and Adelantes. But enough of logic-chopping: McKeen was a major pioneer in the field of the motorised railway. Almost single-handedly he devised and saw through the first large-scale production of purpose-built motor railcars, some 152 of them constructed 1905-1917, most to a standard design or near

3810 Motor Car, La Jolla, San Diego, California
"On the Line of the Santa Fe"

The 'Submarine', a 55 ft McKeen in rich maroon livery for the 'La Jolla Line', Los Angeles, San Diego Beach Railway, at the receiving end of teenage menaces (see text). From an original postcard by Cardinell-Vincent, San Francisco.

variants thereof. The majority operated in the USA, but the McKeens also reached other parts of North America, Europe and Australia.

McKeen's ingenuity went further; he designed a motor shunting locomotive, a half-track road vehicle and a 'balloon support vehicle' - a lorry which could wind down artillery-observation

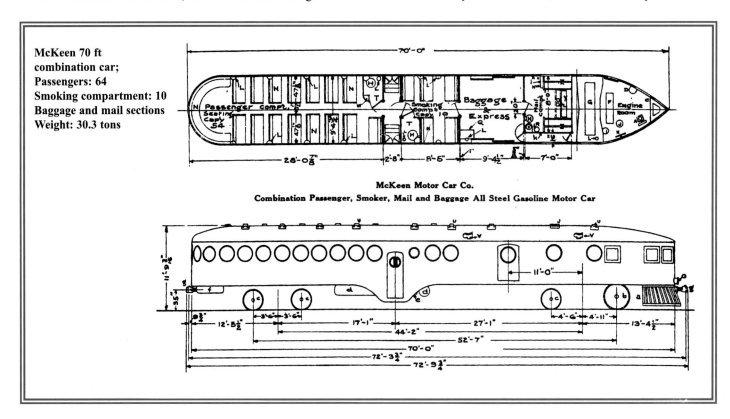

**McKeen 70 ft combination car;
Passengers: 64
Smoking compartment: 10
Baggage and mail sections
Weight: 30.3 tons**

**McKeen Motor Car Co.
Combination Passenger, Smoker, Mail and Baggage All Steel Gasoline Motor Car**

balloons in double-quick time. But the 'McKeen car' for railways was his main achievement.

The McKeen car had great promise and was widely acclaimed initially. It suffered two defects, however. First, it lay at the cutting edge of too many individual technologies, notably in the design of motors, transmission, and body construction. McKeen showed great originality in all these areas. But secondly, he had 'attitude', a fierce temper, and quite as bad, an obstinate refusal to listen to or take advice: more of the Webb tendency than the Churchward one.

He seems also to have been something of a card. Always stylishly and impeccably attired, he worked from an office where the walls were adorned with charming pictures of Gibson girls and Egyptian dancers - emphatically not something one found on equivalent premises at Crewe or Swindon, or Altoona for that matter. He was well-off, the son of an Indiana banker. Following an excellent education which included the Universities of Berlin, and Johns Hopkins, and an American Polytechnic, he rose by dint of high competence to become the UP's motive power chief at Omaha,

Union Pacific 55 ft standard McKeen passenger M-19 on platform 2, Omaha Union station, 10th July 1908 - lady in dropped entrance possibly a McKeen acquaintance.

Nebraska, 1902.

This position brought him to the notice of the road's controlling financier, Edward Harriman. Harriman, one of the wealthiest men in the USA, was no mere financial manipulator. Anxious to make the UP and others of his lines more profitable, he carried out a wide range of improvements including standardised locomotives and rolling stock; time-saving cut-off lines; and centralised procurement systems. In 1904, keenly on the search for cost-

A McKeen transversely-mounted 200 hp petrol engine, cam reversing lever between exhaust manifolds, 42 inch driving wheels in front, 33 inch rolled steel trailing wheels, flywheel in between.

Top: The last word: 70 ft baggage and mail car (M-23) with an uprated 300 hp motor, hauling an all-steel McKeen passenger
          carriage running on ball-bearing axles (with a passing resemblance to later État 'saucisson' carriages); experimental air
          horn on cab roof; Lucin cut-off, 1909.
Above: Refurbished and modernised McKeen sets, M-23 and M-24 in streamline yellow and brown, with petrol-electric propulsion,
          (see exhaust assemblies atop driving ends) and original 55 ft McKeen steel trailers. Photo: Union Pacific RR.

reductions, he warmed to the then fresh idea of motorised railcars and instructed McKeen to design and test one.

The outcome, the M-1, was entirely McKeen's brainchild, the remarkable precursor of his later fleet of railcars. This pioneer was constructed amidst some secrecy at the UP's Omaha shops and outshopped in January, 1905. In March it was tested in Nebraska and California and found to operate successfully. By September it was already in revenue-earning operation.

The 31 ft long M-1 was smaller than the later McKeens, but it bore a strong family likeness, notably its striking 'windsplitter' shape, a long, knife-sharp bow and a rounded stern. To the aerodynamic innocents of the day, without access to wind-tunnel testing, this seemed the obvious configuration. In practice it was not; if anything a McKeen car offered less air resistance in reverse. The M-1 was powered by a Standard 100 hp petrol engine, driving one of the two axles. The next product, the M-2 (September, 1905) was much larger, a 55-ft car able to carry 57 passengers and touch 53 mph. It ran on two bogies, the motor driving the leading axle. Henceforth all McKeen cars used this form of drive.

Improvements continued until the definitive McKeen design was embodied in M-7, 1906. Many creative ideas flowed into these early railcars: pneumatically-operated doors; fresh air circulated on a 4-minute cycle; a variety of interior heating and cooling systems; indirect lighting by acetylene or electricity; air-operated clutches and sharply-dropped entrance doors. The most enduring McKeen trademark was the 22in diameter porthole windows designed to compromise body strength less than the traditional rectangular form and to be dust-proof. Although most McKeens had these windows, a small minority employed the rectangle and arch form instead.

In any case the car body was tough; one-eighth inch steel sheets wrapped around two-inch I-beams, the sheets contributing to overall strength. The result was referred to as a 'unibody' design, en route to the monocoque form, but not of it. Some of these innovations were sound, and caught on. The McKeen bogie, for example, was widely adopted by Harriman's 'Associated Lines'; it was strong and rode comfortably, although its bearings tended to run hot. The porthole windows sealed well, but they swung upwards and inwards and, as their catches wore, they started to swing back involuntarily, sometimes striking passengers. The heating systems were a mixed bag. One form, running off the exhaust, could build up sufficient back pressure to stall the engine. Water heaters working off the engine manifold could not really cope with prairie winters. Eventually conservatism triumphed, and reliable 'Baker stoves' had to be installed.

The classic McKeen car was not only in the technical vanguard. With its round windows and windsplitter prow, its lean profile generally decked out in enamelled maroon set off by black bogies, it was an impressive sight, rather like contemporary views of 'the railway of the future'. The McKeen form might have sprung from the work of an illustrator for H G Wells or Jules Verne.

A turning-point was reached about 1907. For some time McKeen had hankered after designing a dedicated motor for his railcars; this was duly installed in M-8, a 200 hp engine mounted transversely on the front bogie, as with all McKeens. Whether he yearned for greater independence, or had been investing too much time in internal combustion mechanics, or for whatever reason, McKeen parted company with the UP although not with Harriman; the McKeen project consequently remained closely related to the Union Pacific. Harriman set him up as president of the newly-formed McKeen Motor Car Co (1908) following a successful demonstration tour of the M-7 to New York.

The McKeen organisation had a capital of $1m and employed fifty mechanics, mostly ex-UP men. It leased part of the UP Omaha works and received a boost through a large Union Pacific order. Of the 150 or so McKeens built, about 25 were eventually run by the UP, slightly more on the Harriman-controlled Southern Pacific.

The tempting interior of a refurbished UP McKeen trailer, employing former main-line parlour-car furniture. Photo: Union Pacific RR.

Most orders tended to be for smaller batches or one-offs, to about 35 lines in total. Some went to large railroads: Chicago & North Western; Erie; Texas & New Orleans; or Illinois Central, for example. Others went to middle-weights (Chicago Great Western; Oregon Short Line; Ann Arbor) or minor concerns: Hocking Valley; Virginia & Truckee; Salem, Falls City & Western. As McKeen's fame spread, six cars were sent to Queensland, tailored for the 3ft 6in gauge, and two to Victoria (5ft 3in gauge), as well as Cuba, Spain, Canada and Mexico, where they ran on two Harriman-controlled lines.

This was also the era of the 'electric interurbans' some of which, notwithstanding, employed McKeen cars. One, the Minneapolis & Northern, decided to use nothing else when it opened in 1913.

A 1912 catalogue claimed that 124 cars had been sold, which suggests that the McKeen golden age was c. 1908-12. It listed about 170 places which were served by McKeens, mostly by branch, local and secondary services.

The McKeen cars promised to reduce expenses, partly through crew reductions since they required no fireman, and partly by cutting the standby losses which were a problem of the steam locomotive. McKeen realised the need for flexible capacity and designed a fully-portholed all-steel trailer car, 31 ft long. In his UP days he had also designed a remarkable 68 ft main line carriage of similar design, claimed to be fireproof. This long carriage did not catch on but shorter versions, running on roller-bearings, were occasionally seen behind a McKeen car, visions of a future that might have been.

Troubles began to close in on the McKeen enterprise, however. The motor and transmission were difficult to operate and none too reliable. Mounted on a bogie, the vibrating motor punished the track and took hard knocks itself. After the honey-moon period, especially as wear and tear took hold, passengers complained of motor noise, juddering, and exhaust whiffs.

In spite of the trailer experiment, and publicity shots of a McKeen car banking a 40-ton coal wagon up a ramp, the cars lacked the 'general purpose' capability of steam engines. Constructing special mail and baggage versions of the standard car underlined the point. The McKeen petrol shunting locomotive, effectively a car shorn of its passenger accommodation, had few takers.

The McKeen system was also none too popular with organised labour. The saving on crew wages, attractive to capital, was the reverse to them. McKeens were temperamental and often awkward to drive; as unreliability and faults multiplied so did maintenance difficulties. It was remarked that the drivers of these 'cars of the future', having spent hours tinkering with motors and transmission, often had more grimy overalls and hands than their colleagues who sailed by in the cabs of steam locomotives.

McKeen firmly declined to refine his design by body-mounting the engine, or adopting more flexible hydraulic or electric transmissions. Harriman, his main backer died in 1909 and orders fell off, particularly after 1912. The McKeen Co closed its doors shortly after the Great War. But McKeen himself fell on his feet; the ever-supportive UP, the majority shareholder, took care of outstanding debts. Two modified cars were constructed from spare parts and given 300 hp Scott-Hall motors; they lasted on the UP until the 1950s, outlasting McKeen who died in California, 1946.

McKeen mechanics

The heart, and Achilles' heel, of the McKeen car was its motor and transmission technology. A brief description of the starting, stopping and reversing of a McKeen car ought to 'say it all' to readers.

To start a McKeen's six-cylinder, transverse mounted engine, compressed air was admitted into the three right-hand cylinders to get the motor turning. Fuel was then admitted to all cylinders which were fired by magneto. The first magnetos were of German design, firing two plugs per cylinder. Later, the UP in particular used the Duff magneto specially adapted for firing the distillate fuel preferred by McKeeen and the UP. As the engine turned it spun a massive flywheel which could be observed outside the bogie, spinning behind the front driving wheels. There were two gears, low for starting, high for normal work; the final gear ratio was 4:1. The motor, designed for 350 rpm could drive a 35-ton car in favourable conditions at up to 60 mph. Fuel consumption hovered at about 3 mpg.

Transmission was by a cone clutch and chain drive; early clutches were operated by lever, later ones pneumatically. Reversing a McKeen car was a pain. The car had to be stopped, and the motor shut down. The driver then went to the motor and shifted the camshaft so that when it was restarted (by compressed air in the usual way) it ran in reverse; i.e. the motor was reversed, not the gear-train.

Clutches gave plenty of trouble; their design left them either too hard, in which case they imparted a jolt to the motor and passengers, or too soft in which case they wore quickly or burnt out.

There was a small range of body designs around this singular and curious machinery. McKeen offered two car lengths: 55 ft and 70 ft; cars might be purely for passengers or, quite commonly, combination baggage and passenger vehicles, able to take 38 or so passengers in the rear section. There was a 55 ft freight trailer, and a shorter passenger trailer, but no great market for either. In 1913 McKeen tried to break into mainline traffic with a revived 58 ft all-steel trailer hauled by a 70 ft express baggage car with an

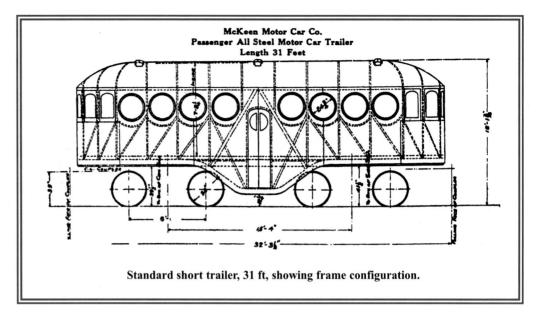

Standard short trailer, 31 ft, showing frame configuration.

uprated standard motor of 300 hp, but the ploy came too late and failed to stimulate trade.

Reflecting prejudices of the time, a Norfolk & Southern 70 ft car had a segregated 'Jim Crow' compartment for black people, the only McKeen car so blighted. The most powerful McKeen, for the steeply-graded Southern Utah Rly, was non-standard, a 58 ft car with duplicate brakes, a 300 hp motor and two driving axles joined with connecting rods. McKeens were adaptable to non-American usages; those running in Victoria, for example, (Ballarat-Maryborough, and Hamilton-Warrnambool) had higher doors and buffing plates to match Australian platforms and buffers.

The sleek appearance of the McKeen car was enhanced by hanging the radiator low, behind a most potent looking cowcatcher. Exhaust was carried away in a long pipe underneath the car, discharging from behind like an automobile. Early cars had a gramophone-like air-horn mounted above the cab, but these proved rather gutless and were replaced by an air-actuated chime whistle.

In later years, when railways could adopt and adapt McKeen cars as they pleased, many were converted to petrol-electric transmission. It was quite common for them to lose their windsplitters at the same time, using interior space more rationally. Latter-day ex-McKeens typically mounted complexes of radiators and exhaust pipes forward, less elegant but more pragmatic than the pre-Great War futurist style.

In Australia, the Victorian McKeens which had arrived amidst

The actual appearance of a standard 70 ft McKeen combination car, Oregon Short Line No. 480, the sleekness offset by a hazardous looking exhaust pipe to the rear.

great fanfare in 1912, shipped in the largest seaborne crates until that time (70ft x 11ft), only lasted for three or so years. Converted to steam trailers in 1919, they were scrapped in 1925. In their homeland, long after the failure of the McKeen Co, many of its cars soldiered on, beneficiaries of the legendary American technical skills; possibly the last in its original form, Virginia & Truckee No. 22 ceased work in 1947, well within living memory.

Legends and lore of the 'Doodlebugs'

There was plenty of McKeen car folklore, then and later. Much of it surrounded the problematic propulsion system. If compressed air leaked away when a car was standing dead, for example overnight, it was impossible to start by the intended means. Not infrequently a McKeen car had to be push-started by the nearest available steam locomotive, usually a shunter ('switcher' or 'yard goat'). Sometimes the plane geometry of a 'wye' or siding might assist with a rolling start, and on one occasion a car was so placed by mule-power, although it rolled away prematurely and struck a mule painfully, happily no worse.

The dread process of reversing was also assisted by turning on favourable wyes, or more commonly, turntables. McKeen quirks included water leaking past gaskets into cylinders, draining the water pump system and leading to overheating and pre-ignition with consequent judders and reports from the motor. On the Los Angeles & San Diego Beach RR, adventurous teenage nuisances, an abiding feature of Western culture, found that by screwing down the handbrake on the McKeen trailer they could overload the motor in the power coach, causing it to 'bog down...and spout like a whale' (Journal of San Diego History, Jan 1961).

On this San Diego line McKeens were dubbed 'Submarines' on account of their shape. But they had many other sobriquets: Bug, Doodlebug, Red Flash and Red Devil, the last two arising from the normal livery finish of rich maroon. 'Doodlebug' was a generic term for motor railcars, applied also to the McKeen's chief rival, the contemporaneous GEC petrol-electric railcars. The uncomplimentary Oregonian term for McKeens, 'Skunk',

may have arisen from the exhaust-fume problem.

Many lines painted McKeens in their own colours. For example, when the UP modernised some in the 1930s it decked them out in its eye-catching 'streamline yellow and leaf brown', just like its new transcontinental motor-powered expresses. The Chicago Great Western reassembled some McKeens into a three-coach luxury motor train, the Blue Bird, 1929, 'America's Premier Deluxe Motor Train', catering especially for patients at the exclusive Mayo Clinic in Rochester, Minnesota.

Image and reality: the McKeen legacy

McKeen himself had been a master of PR presentation, demonstrating that he was ahead of his time in another way at the dawn of our era, the post-modern age when image can overtake reality in importance. When M-7 was sent to New York, McKeen and Harriman laid on a magnificent dinner for financiers. An electric model McKeen car sped around the table, but had to be stopped because it so held the attention of the diners that they ignored the repast spread before them. McKeen worked the press and its photographers hard, reporting new cars despatched to customers in long trains; or sent speeding over the Lucin cut-off. The Omaha shops were opened one Sunday in 1910, well-supplied with guides and musical accompaniment. 'Photo opportunities' were almost commonplace, a newly turned-out car often set off by McKeen with his fierce red beard and striped shirt to match, or his current sweetheart in the elegant attire of the day: long skirt, starched blouse and stupendous hat.

McKeen's 1912 catalogue reinforced this kind of hype with testimonials from users. Some were back-handed: the Southern Pacific noted that steam trains had replaced McKeens because they generated so much traffic, 'more than a motor car could handle'. The Denver, Laramie & North-Western stated that McKeen running costs compared favourably with steam train costs (16.91 cents per mile: 33.92 cpm). The Governor of Sonora, in Mexico, had taken forty friends on a McKeen trip (on another SP subsidiary, the FC Cananea, Rio Yaqui y Pacifico); they found

*The classic McKeen; Union Pacific M-22 (1909) in its later years, an unmistakably American vehicle.
Photo courtesy of Denver Public Library, Western History Department.*

the car 'attractive and comfortable', ideal for 'this hot climate'. J Burlingett, general manager of the St. Joseph & Grand Island Rly reported that the frugal McKeens (12 cpm in this case) put up a 'very creditable' performance. He had even been advised by farmers that the service of the McKeens had 'increased the value of their land'.

But to no avail. Each new generation of politicians, PR experts and spinners has to learn the wisdom of Abraham Lincoln's dictum: 'You cannot fool all the people all of the time'. The ranks of disaffected passengers and mechanics were now joined by operators who knew about mounting maintenance and repair costs, of McKeens lying fallow, awaiting repairs - the sin of idle capital.

The McKeen saga, like many in railway history, is rich with ironies and precepts. Too much poorly-evaluated innovation was combined and rushed into being. McKeen, at once a source of brilliant innovation and mule-headed conservatism, was largely responsible for this state of affairs. In one important and enduring respect neither he not his railcar failed at all. The Doodlebugs may have long gone, but the McKeen concept, volume production of purpose-built, motor-propelled rolling stock, is alive and well. Every Class 158 or Virgin Voyager is to that extent a latter-day witness to the power of McKeen's vision.

References, Further Reading,

References to McKeen cars are many, but scattered. The best overall brief survey can be found in *Trains* magazine, Vol 20, 9, July 1960: 'Knife-noses and Portholes' by William W Kratville. Exhaustive treatment of the McKeen phenomenon, supported by detailed rosters, is in Edmund Keilty, *Interurbans Without Wires* (1979), and *Doodlebug Country* (1982), now rarities. Because of the UPRR role in the McKeen epic, William Kratville and Harold E Ranks, *Motive Power of the Union Pacific* (1958) is an important source. A well-illustrated survey of a typical McKeen one-off can be found in Ted Wurm and Harere Demoro, *The Silver Short Line, A History of the Virginia & Truckee Railroad*, (1983). McKeen references are frequently to be lit upon in individual railroad histories. McKeen's futuristic, all-steel mainline carriage is covered in *The Railway Gazette*, Nov 15, 1907.

The Victorian McKeens are described in *The Victorian Railways Newsletter, 5*, 'Rail Motor Services'; I am indebted to Ian R Barkla, Secretary & Research Officer of the Australian Railway History Society for a copy of this paper and much else besides.

The 'Web' bears a good deal of McKeen material; interested parties might try viewing www.northeast.railfan.net and www.angelfire.com/or/owosso/mckeen.html for starters.

For those who prefer the real thing, the Nevada State Railway Museum is currently restoring the Virgina & Truckee RR 70 ft McKeen, No. 22, taken back into the fold after years as a cafe, and a plumber's office. The story can be read on the museum website, www.nsrm-friends.org/nsrm44.htm

Memo to Iberian railway experts: any light which can be thrown upon the Spanish McKeen/s would be welcome; American sources are a touch laconic about this railcar export.

Made in the DDR -
East German Electric Locomotives Still at Work in China
LEW Henningsdorf Products Stand the Test of Time - *by Nicholas Pertwee*

The events which led up to the re-unification of Germany in 1989 altered not just the political face of the eastern part of the country which, as the German Democratic Republic, had been an independent sovereign state since 1949. This was a foundation date shared with one of its later trading partners, the People's Republic of China, and it is of course with China as an export destination that this article is concerned.

Profound change was also brought about in the erstwhile DDR's industrial sector when companies which had been used to a centralised control system were exposed to Western-style market forces and management methods. Many of them failed to live through this period. Only those which were fundamentally sound and whose products, based on a long tradition of technical excellence, met the exacting standards of potential buyers, were enabled to survive the transition and emerge unscathed. One such was in Hennigsdorf, near Berlin, the former Lokomotivbau-Elektrotechnische Werke "Hans Beimler" (LEW) which rose from the war-time ruins of the old AEG-Borsig factory. It reverted to AEG in 1991 and was then owned by Adtranz / DaimlerChrysler Rail Systems GmbH from 1996. Ownership then passed from them to Bombardier in 2001.

The impressive two-part 'Zeitzeugnisse 1945-1990 - Aus der Geschichte eines traditionsreichen ostdeutschen Industrie-betriebes' (Ref. 1) which appeared in December 1999 as a tribute to one of the pillars of the old German Democratic Republic's industrial establishment provides a remarkably detailed record of its organisation and activities. It will be the indispensable work

for researchers of LEW for years to come and has been drawn on extensively in this survey; specifically, among a host of other things, for technical details and export figures and in relation to the situation that existed in the immediate post-war period. The quality and durability of the firm's products is shown by the fact that they can still be seen at work in many countries, and not just in what used to be member states of the former Comecon bloc, almost invariably in extremely demanding operational and environmental conditions. The oldest examples still at work, the 80-ton Bo-Bo's on the coal-mining railway at Fuxin in China, were built in 1950 and 1951 and the class they represent was the first to come from the works at Hennigsdorf after the war. They have an interesting history and are dealt with in some detail later. They belong in fact to the Class IV KP1.

In the 40 years of the DDR's existence LEW produced a total of approximately 12,500 locomotives of all types, 3,700 diesel and 8,800 electric, both for industrial and mainline use, many of which were exported (Zeitzeugnisse, Part 1, p. 142). It would take a lifetime to track down however many of them still exist but to identify those which went to one particular country might not be such an impossible task, particularly if it was narrowed down to either diesel or electric locomotives and one restricted oneself to the industrial sector. If a distinction was then made between narrow- and standard-gauge engines, then the field is made even smaller. It would be a successful exercise indeed if research into the group that came out of this whittling-down process - standard-gauge industrial electric locomotives, in other words - served to supplement and corroborate the information provided in the works list painstakingly assembled by Ingo Huetter, based on research done by Horst Lauerwald of Nordhausen, and the later version produced by Jens Merte.

Once on the ground things are different from putting together lists on paper and expecting the evidence to fall neatly into place but I believe that sufficient research has been done in coal- and iron-ore mining areas of China to make this a worthwhile exercise for this selected group. The whole picture is not yet clear, but that is no reason not to make a start. Little, to my knowledge, has been published about these engines as most people who visit China are more interested in steam locomotives, the more so as this is now a threatened species even there and attracting more

One of the Fuxin Mining Railway's LEW 80-ton Bo-Bo type IV KP1 Mark IV electrics, no. 6603 which was manufactured in 1951. Fifty years later, in May 2001, it was observed hauling heavy spoil trains at the mine. Photo: Nicholas Pertwee

The EL1 class Bo-Bo-Bo is illustrated by no. 9243 of 1960 seen working at Fuxin. The overhead and side collectors are clearly seen on the roof and mounted in front of the cab, the latter being to allow working in Haizhou open-cast pit. The louvres at the front and rear above the bogie are to allow ventilation to reach the compressors for the traction motor blowers.

Photo: Nicholas Pertwee.

attention than ever for that reason.

But no one person can be the sole repository of any package of information, no matter how specialised, and to achieve even a reasonable degree of completeness many other sources have to be tapped. 'Industrial Locomotives of the People's Republic of China', which has just seen its third addendum, is a distillation of the contributions of many observers of the industrial railway scene and provides a ready-made guide for anyone interested in finding these locomotives. I have referred to it many times in putting these notes together, (abbreviated simply to 'Industrial Locomotives'). It was compiled by R.N. Pritchard and published in 1996 by the Industrial Railway Society. It has been supplemented by three amendment lists, nos. 1, 2, and 3, featuring in IRS Bulletins nos. 671 (July 1999), 694 (Sept. 2000) and 725 (July 2002). The 'Continental Railway Journal', published quarterly by the Continental Railway Circle, regularly carries information about China and though it tends to concentrate on steam, it also covers other types of locomotive, both mainline and industrial.

Based on such sources, my own observations, and personal communications and conversations it first seemed clear that LEW standard-gauge industrial electric locomotives of Classes EL1 and EL2 were to be found at work mainly at the steelworks and iron ore mines, and the ring-railway, at Anshan; coal mines at Fushun and Fuxin; the steelworks at Benxi with its associated iron-ore mine at Waitoushan, all of which are sites in Liaoning Province spread loosely round its capital Shenyang, and on the coal-mining system at Hegang in Heilongjiang Province much farther north. The 1950/51 IV KP1s mentioned earlier work at Fuxin. It would be a highly significant event if any of these were found anywhere else but until that happens Fuxin is almost certainly the only place where they are still in existence as the two that used to work at Anshan have been scrapped (according to information from a veteran railwayman at Anshan steelworks electric locomotive maintenance depot in personal conversation. Regrettably not a single part of them is left as they have been terminally recycled).

But then other locations began to feature again. Visitors to Pingzhuang in Inner Mongolia for instance, according to CRJ and IRS reports, were able to establish that an earlier non-specific reference to "20 or so Fushun-style Bo-Bo electrics" being there in 1994 ('Industrial Locomotives') meant in fact EL2s and that '20 or so' was probably a conservative estimate. Indeed, the actual number on the roster in the summer of 2002 was 37. Qitaihe in Heilongjiang Province is rather more inconvenient to get to than the more established sites and the fact that its coal-mining railway has a small fleet of EL1s and EL2s was only brought up again as recently as 2002 (CRJ no. 130). Another candidate is the Panzhihua Titanium Works in Sichuan Province where an EL2 was seen in 1998, but there is so far no other information to hand from this place. This is the only case so far where no more than a single engine has been seen and it has been assumed that if this is a genuine allocation there are others there as well. The generous apportionment of resources, both human and mechanical, that is a feature of all the industrial sites in China visited personally so far, and their size and scale, suggests that a single engine would hardly be adequate. That the Panzhihua orphan may not be completely neglected is backed up by the implication that exchange sidings or a link with the Panzhihua Iron Ore Mine Railway exist at a common junction point (IRS Bulletin no. 725). In or before 1993 this iron ore mine used 23 electric engines, according to a Chinese source (Ref. 2). Unfortunately a breakdown as to type is not given but seven of them have been seen since and identified as Chinese-made 150-tonners. Despite this it is not impossible that engines from other manufacturers are represented among the balance, and maybe even LEWs.

Nevertheless, for lack of evidence, Panzhihua has been omitted from the following table which estimates the number of standard-gauge LEW electric locomotives allocated to each site. The total number of engines exported to China, or indirectly via the USSR in the case of the IV KP1, is known from LEW publicity material or from Zeitzeugnisse, while the allocation figures are based on numbers or groups of running numbers so far encountered. In the sections devoted to the individual locomotive classes this table has been expanded by adding the number of engines actually seen at the various places, irrespective of their condition. A reasonable number of these have also been positively identified by works number and date but this has not been possible in all

Representing the EL2 class Bo-Bo is one of Anshan's immaculately turned out locos, no. 7220, dating from 1972. The two roof level pantographs have been lowered and the loco is working on the rear side-wire collector. It is just possible to discern the front and rear of the loco numbered as ends 1 and 2 on the frame and the axles are numbered 1 to 4 above each of the axleboxes.

Photo: Nicholas Pertwee.

cases. Only the basic details - format, for instance, or letters written large as with VEM or LEW on the IV KP1's plates - can normally be obtained from engines in motion, and even when they are stationary the state of the plates often means they are illegible.

Descriptions of and comments on the three standard-gauge classes that are to be seen working above ground with details of their technical specifications (Zeitzeugnisse Part II) are provided in separate sections below. It should be added that this by no means exhausts the types of LEW industrial engines exported to China, for battery and overhead-wire 4-wheeled mine engines of classes EL5, EL8 and EL9 were also sent there in large numbers. 'Zeitzeugnisse', in Part II, tells us that in total 740 EL5s were exported between 1951 and 1982, 512 EL8s between 1951 and 1973 and 1510 EL9s from 1952 to 1980 but, though China was one of a number of destinations in each case, there is no numerical breakdown given per country. In their works lists, however, both Huetter and Merte agree that 330 EL5s went to China between 1976 and 1979 and that 200 EL9s were sent there, 105 in 1979 and 95 in 1980. No figures are available for the EL8.

By their nature the battery-powered types, EL5 and EL8, would only be seen above ground in rare instances, mainly when heavy repairs were required, and none have been reported. (Contrary to this though, it is worth mentioning that a former driver of EL5s, now in a management position

OVERVIEW OF LEW STANDARD-GAUGE ELECTRIC INDUSTRIAL LOCOMOTIVES EXPORTED TO CHINA					
IV KP1 80t Bo-Bo WE		**EL 1** 150t Bo-Bo-Bo WE		**EL 2** 100t Bo-Bo WE	
60 exported 1950/51		121 exported 1960/80		186 exported 1957/84	
Location	Allocation	Location	Allocation	Location	Allocation
ANSHAN	2	ANSHAN	35	ANSHAN	60
		FUSHUN	40		
		BENXI	10	BENXI	24
		WAITOUSHAN	(5)	WAITOUSHAN	(5)
FUXIN	58	FUXIN	20	FUXIN	4
		HEGANG	10	HEGANG	46
		QITAIHE	6	QITAIHE	4
				PINGZHUANG	37
				UNKNOWN	11
TOTAL	60	TOTAL	121	TOTAL	186

Notes:

a. Export figures for the EL1 and EL2 are taken from Zeitzeugnisse Part II, p. 104 (EL1) and p. 98 (EL2)

b. The Benxi allocation figures include Waitoushan

c. The IV KP1 was exported indirectly via the USSR. 36 were also built at Hennigsdorf in 1949 but none are known to have been passed on to China by the USSR.

d. In the case of the EL2 there is one works number grouping from which not a single locomotive has been identified so far. There is obviously no way yet of knowing where the 10 in this group were allocated and for the moment that entry will have to remain 'Unknown'. To this has been added the one EL2 seen at Panzhihua, for the reason stated above.

at a mine at Qitaihe where the LEW battery-powered mine engines once worked, said that repairs were actually carried out underground as it was too much of a problem to bring these engines up to the surface once they had been taken down). But neither have any of the overhead-wire models (EL9) been reported and visits to narrow-gauge electric mine railways at, for instance, Hegang and Fuxin, and Fengshuigou near Pingzhuang, have found only Chinese-made examples. One of the main objectives of my 2002 trip to China was to find narrow-gauge LEW mine engines but it fell well short in this respect. It was only in Qitaihe that any trace was found. Here there had been an allocation of 30 EL5s spread among at least three mines. In one of those they had been put aside only 4 years ago and, infuriatingly, scrapped a mere 2 years ago; now Chinese equivalents are used, according to information from Qitaihe. One of the problems was said to be the availability of spare parts and it may be that a similar fate has befallen LEW narrow-gauge engines in other centres, though having seen the robust construction of their standard-gauge counterparts used on the surface one is reluctant to believe that similar building standards were not applied to them too. One would expect a longer service life than the some 25 years the Qitaihe experience would suggest and hopes that the fact that nobody may yet have been to the right places to see them is the correct explanation. Data and photographs of these engines shown to people working in mines in all the other places visited in June and July 2002 drew a blank and the only conclusion one can draw is that they were sent mainly to mines in other parts of the country which have yet to be visited. Whatever the truth is, this remains an area where much research needs to be done.

For reference purposes the table below provides the specifications of these three classes. The histories of the EL1 and EL2 class electrics will follow in 'Diesels and Electrics' volume II.

Reference notes

Ref. 1: I would probably not have been aware of 'Zeitzeugnisse' if it had not been for the generosity of Prof. Dr-Ing. Ekkehard Gaertner of Henningsdorf in giving me a copy. I am also indebted to Prof. Dr. Gaertner for his having taken the trouble, often at great personal inconvenience and during a period of ill health, to engage in personal correspondence and answer numerous questions about electric locomotives made at the LEW factory. 'Zeitzeugnisse 1945-1990' is published by Jahresringe, Verband für Vorruhestand und aktives Alter, Land Brandenburg e.V., Ortsgruppe Henningsdorf with the support of Adtranz-Daimler-Chrysler Rail Systems GmbH and appeared in December 1999.

Ref. 2 'Zhongguo Tiekuang-zhi' (Records of China's Ore Deposits), p. 638. Published by Metallurgic Industry Press, Peking, December 1993. Chief Editor Yao Peihui.

The works plate of LEW IV KP1 no. 6601 of 1951.

SPECIFICATIONS OF NARROW-GAUGE MINE ENGINES EXPORTED TO CHINA			
Category	EL5 Overhead Wire	EL8 Battery Locomotive	EL9 Battery Locomotive
Wheel Arrangement	Bo	Bo	Bo
Length over Couplers	5110mm	4948mm	2790mm
Wheelbase	1800mm	1500mm	630mm
Wheel Diameter	780mm	650mm	430mm
Gauge	900mm	500-600mm	480-600mm/ 750-900mm
Height	1600mm	1700mm	1600mm
Weight	12.0t	7.5t	4.0t
Maximum Speed	25km/h	20km/h	13km/h
Hourly Output	75kW	17kW	8.8kW
Speed at Hourly Output	13.6km/h	8.6km/h	5.7km/h
Hourly Tractive Effort	19.6kN	8.6kN	5.3kN
Continuous Rating	60kW	9kW	4.8kW
Speed at Continuous Rating	14.8km/h	12.3km/h	8.8km/h
Continuous Tractive Effort	14.2kN	2.5kN	1.86kN
Maximum Tractive Effort	29.5kN	19.6kN	10.6kN
Battery Voltage		112V	72V
Battery Capacity		455Ah	455Ah
Number of Notches		9	4
Voltage/Current	220 or 550V DC		
Electric Brakes	Resistance Brakes		

Source: Zeitzeugnisse Part II - EL5 p. 143 (142-151); EL8/EL9 pp. 130&131 (130-137)

LEW Hennigsdorf Industrial Electric Locomotive Exports to China

Year	Works Numbers	Destination	Service Numbers	Type	Gauge (mm)	Class	Service Weight	Total per Year	Cumulative Totals
1950	6569-6597	USSR*	6569-6597	Bo'Bo'el	1524/1435	IV KP1	80t	29	29
1951	6598-6626	USSR*	6598-6626	Bo'Bo'el	1524/1435	**IV KP1**	80t	29	**58**
1957	7713-7728	China		Bo'Bo'el	1435	EL 2	100t	16	16
1960	9211-9250	China	1-40	Bo'Bo'Bo'el	1435	EL 1	150t	40	40
1961	9326-9345	China		Bo'Bo'Bo'el	1435	EL 2	100t	20	36
1961	9346-9369	China	41-64	Bo'Bo'Bo'el	1435	EL 1	150t	24	64
1970	13228	China	002	Bo'Bo'Bo'el	1435	EL 1	150t	1	65
1970	13229	China	001	Bo'Bo'Bo'el	1435	EL 1	150t	1	66
1970	13230-13257	China	003-030	Bo'Bo'Bo'el	1435	EL 1	150t	28	94
1971	13258-13264	China	031-037	Bo'Bo'Bo'el	1435	EL 1	150t	7	101
1972	13604-13611	China	7211-7218	Bo'Bo'el	1435	EL 2	100t	8	44
1972	13963-13994	China	7219-7250	Bo'Bo'el	1435	EL 2	100t	32	76
1972	13995-14004	China	7201-7210	Bo'Bo'el	1435	EL 2	100t	10	86
1951-1973*	N/A	China	N/A	Bo ea	500-600	**EL8**	7.5t	N/A	**N/A**
1974	14019-14024	China	7401-7406	Bo'Bo'el	1435	EL 2	100t	6	92
1974	14234-14250	China	7407-7423	Bo'Bo'el	1435	EL 2	100t	17	109
1974	14256-14262	China	7424-7430	Bo'Bo'el	1435	EL 2	100t	7	116
1977	15258-15308	China		Bo el	900	EL 5	10t/12t	51	51
1977	15427-15436	China		Bo el	900	EL 5	10t/12t	10	61
1978	15510-15529	China		Bo el	900	EL 5/03	12t	20	81
1977	15536-15565	China		Bo el	900	EL 5	10t/12t	30	101
1976	15706-15755	China		Bo el	900	EL 5	10t/12t	50	151
1977	15776-15844	China		Bo el	900	EL 5	10t/12t	69	220
1977	15850-15867	China		Bo el	900	EL 5	10t/12t	18	238
1978	15868-15889	China		Bo el	900	EL 5	10t/12t	22	260
1978	15910-15939	China		Bo el	900	EL 5/03	12t	30	290
1978	15940-16089	China		Bo el	900	EL 5	10t/12t	150	440
1980	16585-16604	China		Bo'Bo'Bo'el	1435	**EL 1**	150t	20	**121**
1979	16630-16659	China		Bo el	900	**EL 5**	10t/12t	30	**470**
1980	16773-16787	China		Bo'Bo'el	1435	EL 2	100t	15	131
1981	16788-16789	China		Bo'Bo'el	1435	EL 2	100t	2	133
1979	16790-16894	China	Should only be 100 units	Bo ea	480-600 or	EL 9	4t	105	105
1980	17040-17134	China		Bo ea	750-900	**EL 9**	4t	95	**200**
1981	17322-17349	China		Bo'Bo'el	1435	EL 2	100t	28	161
1984	17350-17374	China	8401-8425	Bo'Bo'el	1435	**EL 2**	100t	25	**186**

NOTES

USSR*   Class IV KP1 built at Hennigsdorf as war reparations for the USSR and passed on to China from there.   They are now used only at Fuxin.

1951-73*   Of the 512 Class EL8 mine engines built between 1951 and 1973 an unspecified number was exported to China.
EL8   Zeitzeugnisse (Sources 2) tells us in its Part II that they were used in the DDR and, apart from China, also sent to Bulgaria, Poland, Hungary and Czechoslovakia but no breakdown by country is given.

Sources
1. LEW works lists compiled by (a) Ingo Huetter and (b) Jens Merte
2. Zeitzeugnisse - Aus der Geschichte eines traditionsreichen ostdeutschen Industriebetriebes
3. Personal observations

From Russia With Love -
East German Electric Locomotives Still at Work in China
The LEW IV KP1 80-ton Bo-Bo Overhead-and Side-Wire Electric - *by Nicholas Pertwee*

Turning now to a more detailed explanation of the various types, it makes sense to start with the hitherto mysterious class observed in use only at Fuxin, not just because it is the oldest LEW type still in use in China, but also because of its chequered history. As will become apparent from the story which unfolds next, it should be given the designation IV KP1. Principal technical details are as follows.

A picture is worth a thousand words, as the saying goes, and instead of trying to dredge up an appropriate geometrical term to describe what is in effect no more than a simple rectangular body

with sloping top decking (somewhat obscured by the projecting side-boards) and a central tower cab it is simpler from the outset to let the reader form his own impressions from the pictures shown here and on the next page which show the two versions in use at Fuxin today, Mark III and Mark IV. In the absence of any discernible difference - externally at any rate - between the two types, it is not unlikely that this was simply a way of distinguishing between the years of manufacture, with III referring to 1950 and IV to 1951, and did not imply that any changes in specifications had been made. It has been assumed, if only because it

These views of Mk. III nos. 6591 (left) and 6623 (below left) show the features of the left and right hand sides of the locomotive. The leading bogie can be identified by the compensating spring between the two main springs, so that 6591 is displaying its left and 6583 its right flank. The ventilation louvres, two on the left and three on the right, are confined to the machinery space at the rear of the locomotive. Access to the roof is provided by one ladder, on the left hand side. Mid-July is hot even in northerly parts of China and most engines were running with the rearmost hatch doors open. 6583 is pulling one of the trains which provide transportation for the mine workers with passenger accommodation made from converted goods vans.

The Fuxin Mining Railway logo.

would be illogical if they were not also made, that Mark I and Mark II locomotives exist as well. Two prototypes handed over to Russia on 6th August 1949 might be the Mark I, with the rest of that year's production run being the Mark II, some of which Rakov reports as having worked at Krivoi Rog in the Ukraine.

The question of which was the first works number used by LEW after the war is not one that appears to have been finally answered. KP1 works numbers in the context of the numbering system adopted by LEW are discussed elsewhere, in relation to the works lists produced by Huetter and Merte. The IV KP1 works plates are quite different in format from any of the later types, such as used on the EL1 and EL2 for instance, and are lozenge-shaped, not rectangular. This can be seen from the illustrations on pages 70 and 78.

Today 30 of these engines, according to as near as one can get to official sources, are used throughout the mine railway system both on goods trains and also on the passenger trains, consisting of former goods vans converted to provide rather Spartan accommodation, which run as commuter transport for the mine workers. The table "Class IV KP1 on the Fuxin Mining Railway" provided at the end of this section summarises the basic data as to status, employment and numbering it has been possible to assemble about these, and also about the almost as many others that are still in existence but out of use. All are fitted with side collectors. They can therefore work in Haizhou Pit, the massive open-cast coal mine which is the main feature of the operations at Fuxin, where the gradient out is benign enough to allow them to work single-engine even when bringing up loaded trains, though limited to 6 wagons. This load increases to 9 wagons when they are used in tandem and they can sometimes be seen operating this way out of the pit, or on heavy trains taking spoil up to the slag heaps. They have also been seen double-heading with a Škoda but not with an EL1. Another of their duties is to haul explosives trains, whose vans are painted in distinctive black and white stripes.

Judging from the first and last running numbers to have been recorded, at least as many as 56 units once worked at Fuxin. During a visit in May 2001, 48 were seen, 30 of which were actually working

(25) or being routinely repaired (5). The balance were dumped or in various stages of disuse. In July 2002 the figure was 41 in total of which 21 were in use with 8 in the maintenance shops. On the latter occasion though, one storage yard accessed in 2001 was not examined. Assuming no change in the status quo this site could have produced a net addition of 5 to the total seen, based on a comparison of the running numbers encountered on the two occasions, which would mean that at least 46 are still in existence in one form or another.

The table overleaf summarises the assumptions about how many of the IV KP1 were sent from the USSR and where they worked.

Comparison between Mk. IV no. 6623 (upper) displaying its left hand side and Mk IV 6624 its right hand side (lower) shows that the 1951-made locomotives are no different externally to the Mk. III version of 1950. 6623's crew stock up with water before going down in to Haizhou Pit at the bottom of which one hesitates to think how much hotter it is in the summer than up near its edge. Despite that, with cold weather lasting well into spring and starting again in early autumn, there are few opportunities to give the whole locomotive fleet a face-lift, and only a handful did not still show the ravages of winter even in mid-July 2002.

Works Number Group	Date	Number of Units (Mark)	Locations
6659 - 6626	1950/51	58 (III-29 / IV-29)	Fuxin (56) / Anshan (2)
6569 - 6597	1950	29 (III)	Fuxin
6598*	1951	1 (IV)	Anshan (as local no. 819)
6598 (i.e. 6625)	1951	1 (IV)	Fuxin
6599 - 6615	1951	17 (IV)	Fuxin
6616 (i.e. 6626)	1951	1 (IV)	Fuxin
6616	1951	1 (IV)	Anshan (as local no. 820)
6617 - 6624	1951	8 (IV)	Fuxin
6625 (i.e. 6598 Fu)	1951	[1] (IV)	Fuxin
6626 (i.e. 6616 Fu)	1951	[1] (IV)	Fuxin

Comments & Suppositions to the Above Table

1. * 6598   The existence of this locomotive at Anshan, and its works number details, are known from Industrial Locomotives, p. 60. This is important not just because it establishes the boundary between the 1950 Mk. III, up to 6597, and the 1951 Mk. IV, from 6598. Were it not for that sighting, one might have thought that 6598 at Anshan was an aberration - perhaps an engine on loan or one that went there for repairs; there is no logical reason for one unit to have been plucked from within what is otherwise a complete and unbroken series - and that the two there were actually 6627 and 6628 of 1951. This would give a convenient package from the USSR of 60 engines - 6569-6628.

2. The original 6616 went to Anshan and was numbered 820 there. 6626 stayed at Fuxin, but was renumbered as to running number only, retaining its 6626 works plate, and became 6616 to fill the gap left by the departure of the 'real' 6616 for Anshan to keep the numbers at Fuxin in sequence .

3. Similarly, 6625 became Fuxin's 6598, again to fill the gap left by the original 6598's going to Anshan. 6598, when seen dead in 2001, did not have any plates. It was not seen in 2002 and may have been scrapped. This is inconvenient as a 6625 plate on it would have proved the theory nicely. At the same time though, the absence of any evidence means that it cannot now be disproved.

4. The 1950 and 1951 batches most likely arrived from the USSR in two lots, 29 in 1953 and 29 in 1954, which would explain why 6598 has been seen at Anshan and why the other that was used there also comes from the second batch. The reasoning behind this is the idea that Fuxin, having had to use the whole of the 1950 batch when its railway was starting up in 1953, was in a position by the following year to release two engines to Anshan. It would be satisfying if complete symmetry could be achieved between the Mark III's and IV's, with 30 each, but there is unfortunately no evidence yet from sightings elsewhere or from the spread of works numbers to support that. Nevertheless, if the memory of my informant at Anshan depot was at fault, and there were in fact 4 instead of 2 there, then the total number sent from the USSR rises to a more logical 60 and the number range extends to 6628, with 6627 and 6628 having gone direct to Anshan - but never having been seen or identified. I realise this leads to an unbalanced 29/31 split, but so be it.

5. However, Anshan is a large operation and 2, or even 4, surely would not have sufficed and more were needed. Assuming that Fuxin by 1954/55 was not in a position to release any more of its stock with the expansion of its own operations, the reason for the USSR providing an indeterminate number of its own Novocherkassk-built IV KP1E to Anshan becomes clear. As can be seen from the photograph (#18) of a 1955 example of one of these now being used as an oil storage tank at the Dagushan mine at Anshan, it resembles the earlier IV KP1, apart from the absence of the round-ended 'side-boards' and appearing to have a narrower cab without any space for the roof-access ladder mounted on the IV KP1. It still carries its original Novocherkassk works plates.

6. When these locomotives were sent from the USSR has been in doubt until recently. The only information one had previously came from "Glimpses of China" published by the Foreign Languages Press, Peking, in 1958 which had a photograph of LEW Hennigsdorf No. 6620 already at "the Haichow open-cast coal-mine at Fuhsin (sic)." As the only published reference to their presence at Fuxin one had been made aware of, this was significant in confirming that they cannot have arrived there later than that year. It is also important however as 6620 is one of the 5 locomotives that have never recently been seen at Fuxin and there was a theory that they might have worked at the neighbouring Xinqiu Mine. However, with no confirmation that Xinqiu ever operated a separate electric railway, the implication is that all the IV KP1s worked at Fuxin itself.

7. In their LEW works lists, both Huetter and Merte have their group of 80-ton Bo-Bo electric locomotives for the USSR, i.e. the IV KP1, ending at 6641 (though both also put 6630 as being possibly an underground mine engine for Poland), with numbers immediately after that being EL9s for use in the DDR. Though the evidence that has emerged about the war-reparations order does not support the idea that more than 126 of these were built at Hennigsdorf, or that two parallel series with one for China and one for the USSR were made, the 6641 end-point is significant nevertheless.   It adds weight to the idea that Fuxin received the last two-thirds of the 1950/51 batch of 90, and that LEW built more IV KP1s in 1950 than in 1951, possibly even twice as many, as production at Novocherkassk gradually accelerated

Identification

What has led to the conclusion that these engines are from Class IV KP1 and what brought them to China? IV KP1 is after all a Soviet designation for the 160 such engines built at Novocherkassk from 1950-56. Since these engines had been previously regarded as 'unidentified' and it was even suggested that they would probably remain so, the incentive to find out more about them was that much sharper. Much of the background is in fact readily accessible in LEW publications but this is being wise after the event for it was from Hennigsdorf itself that the key to unlock these sources came, in correspondence from Prof. Dr. Gaertner. In a nutshell, they were built for the Soviet Union as war reparations and given to China in the early 1950s when relations between the two countries were still good and the USSR was building the Fuxin mine railway.

Though an engine of this type was illustrated as early as 1967 in an article in 'Deutsche Eisenbahntechnik' (Jahrgang 15, 12.1967), marking the handing over of LEW's 1000th electric industrial locomotive to the USSR, there was no mention of the specific reason for its having been sent there, nor in a June 1974 article in LEW's house magazine 'LEW- Nachrichten' which had another illustration. In each case the engines are clearly recognisable as the type in use today at Fuxin. With the publication of 'Zeitzeugnisse' 25 years later, the war reparations aspect was mentioned and more complete details and technical specifications of these locomotives became available. Photographs of them at work in Fuxin, sent to Hennigsdorf for identification, were also immediately recognised as being of that type. At the same time, though, it was made clear that they were not given an LEW class designation.

One reason for this is probably due to the special circumstances and one-off nature of the order, but a more compelling one is that their class description had already been decided for them. V.A. Rakov (Ref. 1) quite bluntly, tells us, that "the first electric locomotives of Class IV KP1 were made at the Hans Beimler factory (AEG before the war) near Berlin, starting in 1949." The Russians clearly regarded what later became the LEW factory as their own workshop, and indeed it was the property of the Soviet military authorities for a short time after the war before being returned to German ownership.

The USSR's industrial base too was in tatters at the war's end and despite the wholesale plunder of every conceivable item of movable equipment from its zone of occupation in Germany, it is clear that the re-establishment of its industrial electric locomotive production capacity could not at first keep pace with demand. Hence the reason for its having to use the workshops of the old AEG concern, even though they were far from being completely rebuilt, to produce its first post-war examples. One can only speculate about the measures employed by the Soviet Military Government to ensure the success of this production bridgehead in a foreign country miles away from where the locomotives were to be used, but the result was 126 IV KP1 units in total, 36 made in 1949 and 90 in 1950/51.

Nevertheless, Novocherkassk was able to start production just a year behind, in 1950, of virtually the same locomotive, differing only in the construction of the frames and from then on made a total of 160, as shown in the table opposite (source: V.A. Rakov 'Locomotives of Domestic Railways 1845-1955' 2nd edition, Moscow Transport 1955.

1950	10
1951	13
1952	15
1953	25
1954	32
1955	35
1956	30

Whether the USSR was actually in a comfortable position to release nearly 60 of the Hennigsdorf-made engines to China in 1953-54 without jeopardising its own needs is a border-line matter though the fact that no further imports from Germany were made after 1951 indicates that a balance, precarious though it seems to have been, was struck by then between the Hennigsdorf and the local product. The 1949 batch from Hennigsdorf was obviously all absorbed and at first all the 1950/51 batch was put to use. As we can see, Novocherkassk started up in 1950, but with only 10 engines, and gradually increased its rate of production, but even by 1953/54, despite some degree of overlap with the Hennigsdorf imports from early in its production cycle, Novocherkassk had really done no more than build a roughly equivalent number of their own IV KP1. In other words, they probably had to keep back 30 of the 1950/51 batch for their own purposes even at that stage. The ones they did release can only have been used in the USSR for two or three years and so reached China in almost new condition. Looking at the above figures one has to draw the conclusion that the factors that led the USSR to make this gesture were political just as much as economic. Having said that, there was an ulterior motive too, for in exchange for this kind of technical assistance the Chinese were not slow to 'donate' large quantities of foodstuffs to the USSR, which resulted in many Chinese at the time going hungry.

One of the Mark IV KP1Es made at Novocherkassk without the rounded-end side panels. It was out of traffic and serving as an oil storage tank at Anshan in July 2002.

So, Fuxin's IV KP1s were passed on by the Soviet Union to China as development aid and came from the 1950/51 batch of 90 - probably the last two-thirds. Further evidence of this time when Soviet-Chinese friendship and co-operation were at a high pitch is still to be seen on the mine railway in the form of signals with Russian maker's plates ('Svetofor') on them, dated 1954 and 1955, while in storage in yards at Fuxin itself and at neighbouring Xinqiu there are also Soviet tracked bucket dredgers to be seen, with CCCP prominent on their sides. The IV KP1s would only have needed a change of gauge downwards, and different couplings, for them to be easily transferable. Neither is a particularly difficult technical operation.

Veterans of the railway at Fuxin remember the engines coming from the USSR and official local sources put the dates of their arrival at 1953/54, the likely date of construction of the railway. One has only to go up into the cab of one of these engines to see evidence of their stay in the USSR, in the form of operating instructions in Russian. Remarkably, these are still in place even after the passage of nearly 50 years, some in their original form, some painted over and tags with the Chinese equivalent stuck on top of them. Only their VEM and LEW works plates point to their German origin. The feature that strikes the eye first is a notice above each cab door, on the inside, advising 'Maximum permissible speed 72 kph' and there is also a control panel referring to, and for engaging, such functions as, cabin lighting, heating, compressor No. 1 and No. 2, buffer lights and so on. There is a name tag in Russian for each function and alongside each one a stylised illustration of the feature concerned. Having established where they are situated in the cab, the 72 kph signs in particular were easy to spot from the appropriate angle from outside and were then readily visible in a number of other engines, especially as they are painted yellow. Once the right question was asked, many men old enough to have been there at the time confirmed that they came from the USSR, as part of the package when the Russians built the mine railway. Perhaps it is just as well that one was not aware of this earlier. The need for research would not have been so great, it is true, but much of the interest involved would have been lost as a result.

Provenance

The question of how these engine were produced in such a short time in very difficult conditions is an intriguing one.

Despite the pressure that was obviously applied by the Soviet Military Administration in its zone of occupation to have war reparations obligations made good, it is something of a mystery that Hennigsdorf was able to produce this new type of locomotive in such a short time, all the more as the wholesale removal from this, and other factories, of heavy manufacturing plant to the USSR had stripped it of virtually all the equipment needed for such an undertaking (Ref. 2). We learn from 'Zeitzeugnisse' that to complete this order, which was actually the catalyst for re-introducing electric locomotive construction to Hennigsdorf and setting the operation back on its feet, the entire resources of the firm both human (particularly difficult as there was a huge shortage of, for instance, experienced welders) and mechanical

had to be brought into play. That extraordinary efforts had to be, and obviously were, expended is not in doubt but one cannot help but feel that something more tangible than brawn and determination was needed to design and manufacture from scratch a new model of electric engine in the short time allowed. After all, the factory had only just managed to re-erect some of its buildings after their almost total wartime destruction so that by the end of 1949 the operation had been rebuilt as to 30% (11) and for that reason had been forced to restrict its immediate post-war activities to repairing steam engines and producing agricultural machinery. The order to produce 126 80-ton locomotives was given by the Soviet military administration at the beginning of 1948 and despite the initial lack of appropriate production capacity, to the extent that an essential piece of heavy equipment had to be brought from Hamburg across Zone borders, the first two units were tested and handed over in August 1949 and by the end of that year 34 more had been completed.

Possible explanations are either that (i) AEG had already been designing or producing an engine of this or a similar type before the end of the war, or (ii) the plans or maybe even an intact example or parts of it had survived the bombing, or (iii) the design and possibly components were supplied from elsewhere to assist LEW in the construction, or (iv) a combination of any or all of these was employed.

In support of (i) an article in the October-December 1943 'Elektrische Bahnen' illustrates an 85-ton (100 tons service weight) Bo-Bo engine made by AEG with a distinctly similar outline to the 80-tonners at Fuxin, especially where the 'side boards' with rounded ends are concerned. This differs from the Fuxin models in a number of respects - two pantographs, one each on the fore and aft decking, instead of one; the fact that it is 1,190mm longer than them at 14,310mm and is an altogether larger engine in terms of other dimensions; 30 tons maximum tractive effort compared to its smaller counterpart's 23.5 tons - but the general impression is not at all dissimilar.

Possibly more directly relevant though as a forerunner, given the distinctly antique-looking appearance of the IV KP1, is AEG's model TWL 7113 which appears in 'Die Werkbahn' in a series of articles published in the 1920s (Jahrgang 1925, Heft 14 & Heft 21). The distinct similarity of outline of this early locomotive, which was put into service in May 1924, to the IV KP1 is clearly seen in the illustration from 'Die Werkbahn' shown below.

That there are instances of pre-war designs having been

carried over into the post-war years is not in doubt. The first post-war issue of AEG's house magazine 'AEG-Mitteilungen' (Jan/Feb 1951) has a picture of this same type of engine in action on its cover. It is even the same engine as was illustrated in 1943 in 'Elektrische Bahnen' and bears the same number, 302. Similarly, a mine engine for rack and adhesion drive which is identical in virtually all its external characteristics to LEW's EL14, first produced in 1953 for mines in the DDR and illustrated in Part II of 'Zeitzeugnisse' on page 141, can be traced back to early 1940 (AEG-Mitteilungen Jan/Feb 1940).

Disappointingly, however, my theory expounded in (ii) that parts, or even complete locomotives, survived the war to be used again has to be ruled out, according to Prof. Dr. Gaertner. This being the case, it is hardly likely that items as destructible as plan drawings would have survived the bombing raids either.

However, where (iii) is concerned, the USSR in 1935 was already building Bo-Bo electric shunting engines externally very similar to the IV KP1, even to the extent of the ladder giving access to the roof, as can be seen from a plan drawing seen in a 1952 issue of 'Elektrische Bahnen' (reproduced below). With an overall length of 12,200mm, bogie wheelbase of 3,000mm, and a kingpin centre of 5,000mm they are smaller than the IV KP1, but with their single pantograph on the roof of a centrally-placed tower cab, they actually resemble them more closely than AEG No. 302. It could be the case that the plans for these engines were provided to accelerate production, which might also have been assisted by retained knowledge and experience gained from building the class represented by AEG No. 302, or indeed the earlier models from the 1920's, and we do know from 'Zeitzeugnisse, Part II' that certain components were supplied by the USSR which would have served to speed things up. These include traction and auxiliary motors, compressors, generators, couplings, and wheel sets and axle boxes.

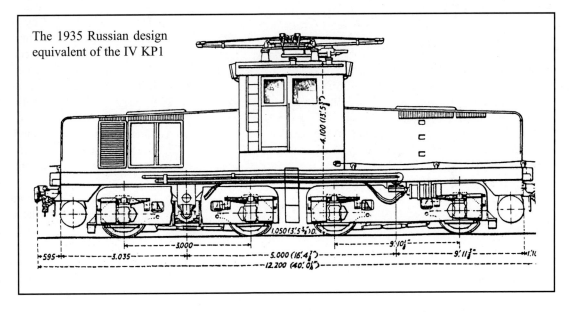

The 1935 Russian design equivalent of the IV KP1

The Numbering System

The service numbers of the engines still to be seen in various forms today range between 6569 and 6626 and it is clear that the system adopted was to have the same running number as the LEW works number. This rule, only broken once with 6626, can easily be established by examining the engines that still have their plates - there are unfortunately some that have no plates at all, or else have had the original VEM (1950) or LEW (1951) plate replaced with, or possibly simply covered up by, a Chinese cabside badge - and going by the ones I have been able to look at closely enough the running number and the works number are the same in all cases except one, 30 out of 31, virtually 100%, or just short of 60% of the total still in existence. The exception (No. 6616 whose plate has Nr. 6626/IV of 1951) is irritating as a sequence breaker on the one hand but it also serves to bring the total number sent from the USSR closer to a more understandable round number of 60 rather than an unsatisfactory 58.

Having first thought that all 90 engines of the 1950/51 production run were sent to China, with the Soviet Union having begun its own production at Novocherkassk in 1950, the complete lack of evidence so far of their existence from any other site in China apart from the two or so that were used at Anshan leads one to believe that the total was more likely to have been 60. Regrettably though, no concrete information about this important point is likely to come from official local sources, and so the best one can do is work on the basis of, hopefully, reasonable assumptions derived from one's own and other observers' experiences on the ground.

LEW Works Numbers and the Fuxin IV KP1

The compilers of the two LEW works lists I have seen (Ref. 3) have based their work on the premise that the first post-war works plate would have had the number 6428. The reason for this is that the last AEG number before the war's end was 6427. We know, however, (from 'Deutsche Eisenbahntechnik' 9/1959) that the order from the Soviet Military Government in 1948 for 126 80-tonners provided the impetus for resuming electric industrial locomotive production. For capacity reasons Hennigsdorf had been forced to restrict its activities up to then to repairing steam locomotives and making agricultural equipment.

This means that unless a new works number was given to the steam engines repaired between 1946 and 1949 (Ref. 4), and to all the pieces of agricultural machinery made, the first post-war number will be carried by the first 'conventional' engine produced after 1945 - which was the first of the IV KP1 order for the USSR, or more specifically the first of the group of 36 made in 1949. Obviously this number is 36 units back from the first of the ones made in 1950 but it is perhaps not as simple as saying that the base number for this calculation is 6569, the earliest number seen at Fuxin. But if it is, and the 90 built in 1950/51 started at 6569, then the first post-war number is 6533. Similarly, the last LEW IV KP1 should be numbered 6658 on this basis, but this does not match with the information provided in the Huetter or Merte works lists, as has been commented on earlier.

'Zeitzeugnisse' does not tell us how many of the IV KP1 Hennigsdorf produced in 1950 and how many in 1951 but if the ideas set out earlier about the circumstances in which the USSR gave these locomotives to China are correct, then Fuxin received the last two-thirds of the 1950/51 batch. That batch's first number would then be 6540 (assuming here for a moment a 60:30 rather than a 58:32 apportionment as postulated earlier) and the first post-war number 36 back from that - 6505.

This in turn would fit in conveniently with the 6630 in both Huetter's and Merte's lists, which is a unit of a completely different class, and to a lesser extent with the fact that their listing for the 80-tonners for the USSR - the IV KP1 in other words - stops at 6641.

References

Ref. 1 "Lokomotivy Otechestvennykh Zheleznykh Dorog 1845-1955" (Locomotives of Domestic Railways 1845-1955), 2nd edition, Moscow Transport 1995.

Ref 2 A fascinating insight into the scale and duration of this exercise is provided by "Kolonne - Die Deutsche Reichsbahn im Dienste dur Sowjetunion" by Michael Reimer, Lothar Meyer and Volkmar Kubitzki, Transpress, Berlin, 1998. This book also has a telling photograph by H. Hensky on p. 7 of one of the erecting shops at Hennigsdorf in 1947 - stripped bare.

Ref. 3 Ingo Huetter and Jens Merte have produced separate versions of the LEW works list which have proved invaluable in tracing the later batches of LEW engines exported to China, but information about the IV KP1 has been patchy even in LEW's own in-house publications and this has made it difficult to record it accurately. This has led to two different approaches. One list omits them altogether, while the other has in effect recorded them twice, with one group assigned to the USSR and another to China. This has resulted in the number of such locomotives produced by LEW in 1950 and 1951 being overstated.

Ref. 4 The first steam locomotive repaired after the war left Hennigsdorf and was handed over to the DR in March 1946. No figure is available for the number of steam locos repaired up to 1949, but 120 were put back into working order up to June 1951.

VEM works plate Nr. 6593/III of 1950.

LEW works plate Nr. 6603/IV of 1951.